MW01196804

Sharon Feanny's
# LIVE FIT KITCHEN

Sharon Feanny's

# LIVE FIT KITCHEN

100 Simple, Delicious Recipes for
Living Fit, Living Life, and Living Love

LIVE FIT
PRESS

Published by Live Fit Press, Montego Bay, Jamaica

Edited and designed by Girl Friday Productions
www.girlfridayproductions.com

Cover and interior design: Rachel Marek
Editorial: Alexander Rigby, Kirsten Colton,
Michael Townley, Kari Somerton
Image credits: cover photos © Sara Lazio;
interior photos © Sabriya Simon, © Sara
Lazio, and © Suki MacDonald Kapahi

ISBN (hardcover): 978-1-7328045-0-0
ISBN (ebook): 978-1-7328045-1-7

To my beautiful children, Toby, Elias, and Noa. I made this book for you so you could have something to show your children. Thank you for being you and for inspiring me every day to be a better person. May you always remember to Live Fit, Live Life, and Live Love, and whatever you do, leave the world a better place than you found it. I love you forever, your Mummy.

Noa's No-Bake Oatmeal, Peanut Butter, and Chocolate Chip Squares, page 207

# Contents

# Recipes

## Snack Time

## Dinnertime

Miss Neng, I could not have done this without you. Thank you!

# Acknowledgments

My heartfelt thanks, love, and appreciation to those who made this book a reality.

There are so many people to thank, but first of all: Miss Neng, this book and the work that I do would not have been possible without you. Fifteen years ago you came all the way from the Philippines to help me raise Toby when I was a single mom. Soon after, I was married again, and we spent endless hours in the kitchen, making healthy meals for my growing family, for friends, and for legendary dinner parties. Then came those famous Shakti bars we created for Shakti Mind Body Fitness, my yoga and fitness center that was my life for so many years, and more recently, when I started doing detox programs, experimenting and perfecting gluten-free, vegan, high-vitality recipes that are now a part of this beautiful book. I may have created the recipes and had the ideas, but it was you, Miss Neng, who really produced the food, day in and day out, not just for my family but also for the countless people we have served over these last few years through my detox programs, cooking workshops, and yoga retreats from our tiny kitchen at home. This is how the Live Fit Kitchen was born. No matter how much work we had ahead of us, or how tired we were, we began each day by saying, "This is the best day of my life," then burst into laughter or a spontaneous happy dance—and from there we got the job done. Words cannot express my deep gratitude for having you by my side every step of the way and for doing it all with such grace, an extraordinary willingness to learn, and a genuine desire for others to receive love through your hands. It's been an unforgettable journey of learning, laughter, and serving others with our gifts. I owe it all to you. Thank you for being there for me, for my family, and for each person that has benefitted from our food. May you be showered with abundant blessings, great health, and soon make your way back home to be with your family.

The list goes on. To my darling Tammy Hart, my BFF, who gave me a Kundalini kick in the butt that helped me get unstuck and finally finish this book. To Laura Darkstar, who held my hand during the painstaking editing process, and to the wonderful team at Girl Friday Productions, led by Alexander Rigby, who believed in me and helped me birth this masterpiece.

To my super-talented photographers, Sabriya Simon, Sara Lazio, and Suki MacDonald Kapahi, for the absolutely gorgeous photos of the food, shot on location at Shakti Home, my om away from home, and little piece of paradise in Treasure Beach. To David Pinto of Pinto Pottery for his one-of-a-kind handmade bowls used in the photos that I treasure and that make everything taste better. To the amazing Robyn Fox, my partner in health who helped me launch my line of Live Fit Kitchen foods by delivering them door to door in Kingston with her impeccable service and genuine care. To my crew on the ground, Emily Albee, James (a.k.a. Lass) Saddler, Tess Dela Cruz, and Opal Grant, you are such an incredible team, always holding the fort—Miss Neng and I could not have done it without you. To Monique Lawrence, you have been there from the beginning and have helped me grow this brand to where it is today—thank you! To my amazing husband, Nicky Feanny, who has been so patient, so kind, and so supportive as I navigated my way across the unknown waters of writing a book. There were so many days (and sleepless nights) when I wanted to jump ship, but you kept me on course. You are my rock. You are my life. Toby, Elias, and Noa, thank you for allowing me to open up our hearts and our home to so many people and for encouraging me every day to keep on going. My daddy and mommy, Peter and Joan McConnell, even though I know you did not always quite understand what I was doing, you were always there for me, cheering me on from the sidelines. I love you both so much. And last but not least, for my Shakti yoga students and those who have been through my detox programs and cooking workshops and kept asking me for recipes, thank you . . . you inspired me to do this. I did it for you.

Finally, thank you, God, for this never-ending gift of yoga in my life. I truly do not know where I would be without it. I am truly blessed. Thank you, thank you, thank you!

May this food nourish your soul and help you Live Fit, Live Life, and Live Love.

# Foreword

Dear Friend,

Thank you so much for purchasing my Live Fit Kitchen cookbook. I welcome you to a high-vitality life! For me, a high-vitality life means having enough energy, health, and passion to live your best life, a life of fulfillment and joy. This cookbook was born out of my desire to share everything I know about living fit, living life, and living love, which is my mantra. The first is always live fit, because if you are not healthy and happy, how can you truly live life to the fullest—and even more importantly, live and share love?

In this book you will find recipes that I created for my Live Fit Detox Programs, yoga retreats, and high-vitality cooking workshops, but are also just what I love to eat every day. If you spent the weekend at our home, this is the type of food you would get: simple, delicious, supernutritious, high-vitality foods that you can prepare for you and your family—with the added bonus that it's food that will help you to feel healthy, happy, and full of energy. I am so excited to share these recipes with you.

My belief is that we all need to be eating foods from the earth that are as fresh and organic as possible. The less we eat out of bags, boxes, and cans, the better for the planet and for us. You will find that most of my recipes contain ingredients that are locally sourced, easy to find no matter where you live, and prepared from scratch.

I wrote this book for you because I am encouraging you with all my heart to move toward a more plant-based life. A plant-based diet does not mean you have to give up meat, but that you choose to focus more on fruits, vegetables, nuts, and seeds: foods from Mother Earth. Not only does this help to prevent chronic diseases (high blood pressure, high cholesterol, high blood sugar, obesity, and cancer), but eating less animal protein is also just better for the planet. Did you know that twenty servings of vegetables produces fewer greenhouse gas emissions than one serving of beef? A plant-based diet requires only one-third of the land needed to support a meat and dairy diet. Adopting a plant-based diet is one of the simplest ways we can reduce the strain on Mother Earth and her precious resources.

One strategy that helps me is that I eat animal protein only once per day. So, for example, if I have chicken or fish for lunch, my dinner would be a vegetarian soup or salad. If I know I'm going out for dinner, I'll have a plant-based lunch. Most days, I don't have any animal protein at all. My body actually tells me when it could do with a little grilled fish, and I listen! This new way of eating has helped me to feel lighter, leaner, healthier, and more energetic—and I hope it will do the same for you.

I want to say a huge thank-you to my amazing cook from the Philippines, Neng Valensoy. Without her, this cookbook would not be possible. Miss Neng, as our family affectionately calls her, has been cooking with me for the past fourteen years. Neither of us are trained chefs. In fact, we started out not having a clue what to do in the kitchen! What we did know is that when people ate our food they felt better, they looked better, and they had a glow, and that made us feel very good. Together we have fed thousands of Live Fit Detox Meals to people doing our Live Fit Detox Programs, and each and every dish was infused with love. In fact, no matter how we are feeling, when we are preparing meals for others, we start our day by saying, "This is the best day of our lives!" We say it over and over until we can feel it in our hearts and our hands, and then we get to work. When you infuse your food with love, it just tastes better. Together, Miss Neng and I created these recipes with much trial and error and a whole lot of laughter and fun. It has been a beautiful journey. I would also like to thank my wonderful family for allowing me to slowly transform our kitchen into a high-vitality energy center and our home into a place for living life and living love where all are welcome!

I welcome your feedback on the recipes and invite you to come to one of my Live Fit Detox Programs, cooking workshops, retreats, or online courses one day. For more information and to sign up for my Live Fit newsletter, please visit www.sharonfeanny.com.

These recipes are given to you with all my love. May they inspire you to take care of you, so that you can be the best that you can be. Enjoy, share, and have fun!

Live love,

Sharon

Berry Delicious Antioxidant Smoothie, page 30

# Introduction

People always ask me what I eat, and many often assume that because I'm a Yogi, I am vegetarian or vegan. It took me a long time to figure out how to describe how I eat to fuel my Live Fit lifestyle, but finally one day it clicked: I eat a high-vitality diet! For me, that means I eat mostly plant-based foods (with occasional naturally raised chicken or freshly caught fish) that are unprocessed, sourced locally, prepared simply, and organic when possible.

## My Journey to a High-Vitality Life

I've always considered myself a healthy person. After all, I'm a yoga instructor and recognized "health guru," and I've owned a yoga and fitness center for many years. But it was not until 2012, when I found myself stressed, terribly depressed, and sick to my stomach (literally) that I really transformed not only how I ate, but also how I lived my life.

Ever since I was a little girl, I've been obsessed with health, nutrition, and wellness. I spent hours in the garden at Worthy Park Estate, my parents' farm deep in the interior of Jamaica, where I grew up, tending to my vegetable patch—and yes, talking to the fairies I saw in the flowers in my mother's magical garden and hanging with my imaginary pet frog, Ucop. No rolling of eyes here, please. As a teenager, instead of dance parties I used to have spa parties, during which my friends came over for weekends of yoga, healthy meals, spa treatments concocted in the kitchen, and long walks in nature.

When I was fourteen, my parents sent me away to boarding school, as is customary when you live on an island. I went from a strict, all-girl Catholic convent to a racy coed school where I was way out of my comfort zone. I was fortunate to make a friend who invited me home for the weekend, as she felt sorry for me because I was so homesick; her mom took me to my first yoga class. This was the first time that I truly experienced that peace is something inside you and always available. This was the beginning of my yoga journey.

I began to read everything that I could find about yoga (which was not much in those days), and I practiced yoga as often as I could throughout the remainder of high school and in college. In 1986, right after graduation, I hitchhiked across America from Florida to Alaska, then traveled to Hawaii, where I became a certified aerobics instructor thanks to a course called "Strong, Stretched, and Centered." During this time I was also exposed to all different styles of yoga, Tai Chi, and raw food. In the three months of this course, I literally transformed my body and mind. I was no longer a self-conscious and insecure young woman. I was confident, self-assured, and ready to take on the world.

This led me to my job as spa director at Sans Souci Hotel and Spa in Ocho Rios, Jamaica. After many more interesting adventures (that I'll save for another book), I went on to work in Newport Beach, California, and eventually ended up back in Jamaica to take a job as the head of public relations for Sandals Resorts.

Throughout this journey, yoga was the stabilizing force in my life. In 1995 I decided to trade my Ann Taylor suits and high-heeled shoes for yoga pants and bare feet—I became a certified yoga instructor at the Kripalu Center for Yoga & Health and an aromatherapist with a vision to heal the world. My dream was to return to Jamaica and share the gift of yoga with everyone I encountered.

Soon after completing my certification, I did return to Jamaica and moved back into my parents' home, where I began teaching free weekly yoga classes to the farmworkers and people in the village. At the same time, I created Starfish Oils, the first-ever line of aromatherapy products for the hotel industry in the Caribbean, which I eventually sold to fund my dream of owning a yoga center in Kingston, the capital of Jamaica.

As with many things I have done in my life, the Shakti Yoga Center (later renamed Shakti Mind Body Fitness) was way before its time. Shakti began in 2000 as one small yoga room with a big dream to bring yoga to Jamaica. A few years later that dream became a large multiroom space offering an array of yoga, spinning, and fitness classes that was, for many, not just a gym but a spiritual center where attendees could grow, learn, laugh, cry, share, dream, and just be themselves. Shakti was a place of refuge for Jamaicans from all walks of life. It was a very special place.

But I chose to close Shakti Mind Body Fitness in 2012, which turned my whole universe upside down; Shakti was my baby, my heart and my soul.

Three years prior to closing, my husband had taken a job in Montego Bay on the other side of the island, and I stayed in Kingston with our three children (my youngest, Noa, was only six months old at the time). Being apart for the first year was OK; somehow I managed the three kids and running a full-time business—I felt like superwoman! By the end of the second year, I began to feel the exhaustion, the separation, and the beginning of a nagging digestive problem that no medication would help. By the third year, I knew for my family and for my health, I had to make a change. I moved to Montego Bay to be with my husband.

Moving to Montego Bay meant closing Shakti, leaving a huge void in my life and in the lives of so many people in the spiritual and fitness community. We had been in operation for over a decade, and during that time Shakti became a trailblazer in the health-and-wellness scene in Jamaica, opening the doors for yoga, meditation, and other healing modalities to a more mainstream audience. By the time I decided to shut Shakti's doors, I realized that although it was serving many people, it was no longer serving me. I had to let my baby go.

For months after closing Shakti, I felt lost. I didn't know who I was anymore. Even though our family was finally united and we were living under one roof after three years of being apart, I felt lonely and depressed, and my stomach problem was out of control. Unfocused and exhausted most of the time, I was drinking four cups of coffee to wake up in the morning and wine every evening to relax, plus I was taking medication to help my acidic stomach and sleeping pills every night. Most of all, I hated how I looked in the mirror. At forty-seven I felt old. I was miserable. I was not happy. Something had to change.

Then, with guidance from Dr. Tracey Wright, a talented chiropractor and health advocate, now forever friend, whom I met at a yoga conference and who ended up living with my family for six months, I put myself on a forty-day detox. I'd done many juice fasts and crazy diets in the past, most of which involved starvation, but I'd never done a detox that allowed you to eat real food. Slowly, I let go of all the foods that were no longer serving me (caffeine, sugar, alcohol, wheat, gluten, and dairy) and started eating only organic, high-vitality foods. I got back in the kitchen with Miss Neng and started to prepare food for my family again. I got really present with my husband and children. I slowed my yoga practice down to restorative yoga and bought a BioMat (a mat that contains crushed amethyst crystals and is heated by infrared light, which helps to speed up the detox process). I rekindled my meditation practice and listened to self-empowerment gurus. I journaled. I rested when I was tired. I ate when I felt hungry. I spent time in nature. I practiced radical self-care. I cried. I laughed. I let go, and after forty days I was me again. Not only did I feel like myself—the strong, passionate, vibrant, positive Sharon that I knew—but I looked like myself again: sexy, glowing, and lean with heart wide open and mind buzzing with ideas and excitement! And that nagging stomach problem? It was gone and replaced with a flat six-pack, and I could rock my yoga pants again. I was back.

In those forty days, I realized that my mission to bring yoga to Jamaica was complete. It was now time to help people to truly live fit, live life, and live love! What if I had just allowed myself to wallow in my sh——? What if I had given into those bad habits? What if I had stopped seeing the unicorns, dolphins, and beauty in life? What if I had let fear close my heart and not believed in love? I had done something that radically changed my life—what if I could help others do this too?

So, being the passionate, purpose-driven entrepreneur that I am, I began putting it out to the universe. I offered my first seven-day detox, then a twenty-one-day detox, and another and another, refining the program each time. I saw the most amazing transformations in the people that really committed to my program. Not only did they change their bodies and their health, but they gained tremendous knowledge, radically increased their confidence, and changed the lives of those around them too. This change in me created a movement. That one drop in the lake has blossomed into a ripple that is spreading across Jamaica and around the world. Today I can say that thousands of people like you are living fit, living life, and living love by just saying yes and trusting in the process. Just imagine if you and everyone around you were operating on this level. What an incredible place this world would be. Sickness would be replaced with vibrant health and energy, life would feel abundant and exciting, and fear would be replaced with love!

Today I share my journey with you and with thousands of others in Jamaica and across the globe through my Live Fit Detox Programs, cooking workshops, yoga retreats and classes, and online courses with the intention to inspire every person I meet to lead healthier, happier lives too. You see, it's not just about what you eat or how you exercise—it's about how you live your life and the choices you make.

What I share with you in this book is raw, real, honest, and still not perfect. I'm not a

## TRY A SEVEN-DAY DETOX PROGRAM

My seven-day detox programs *do not ever* involve starvation or powdered shakes and pills, but rather balanced, healthy, high-vitality meals that are fresh and as organic as possible. The ingredients are grown close to home (that's why I have my own little organic vegetable garden) and provide all the protein, carbs, healthy fats, phytonutrients, vitamins, minerals, and fiber your body needs to feel amazing. On my detox, you even get to eat chocolate! Chocolate, like coffee in its purest form, is actually good for you. It's all about balance and moderation for me.

trained chef or a certified nutritionist, but I'm going to give you everything I have because I have lived it. I want to share my experience with you and with every person I encounter because it is important. Stop the blaming and complaining. Like Gandhi said, "Be the change you wish to see in the world."

## My 80-10-10 Rule That I Follow 80 Percent of the Time

People always ask me what and how I eat, expecting to hear a strict set of rules and regulations on which I base my diet. The truth is, though, the only time I ever really restrict my diet is when I do a personal detox. The rest of the time I adhere to a simple technique that allows me to enjoy food and all the events that come with it, as well as live a healthy and vibrant life. The secret is in my 80-10-10 rule that I follow 80 percent of the time—it's super easy to follow and you can follow it too.

The 80-10-10 rule means that typically my plate consists of 80 percent plant-based foods, 10 percent protein (hormone-free chicken, fresh fish, or legumes), and 10 percent complex carbohydrates (yams, breadfruits, brown rice, green bananas, or quinoa) with a side of healthy fats (avocado, nuts, or seeds). Many people are surprised when I tell them that I eat chicken and fish! I describe my diet as mostly plant-based, but as an avid exerciser and a Yogi, having some animal protein in my diet is what works for me. The Jamaican plate and the standard American diet is usually 80 percent carbs (not the complex ones either), 10 percent protein (usually fried and covered in salty gravy), and a couple tomatoes and shredded cabbage if you're lucky!

I follow these guidelines 80 percent of the time. That means I'm not perfect and some days I want (need) my glass of wine and my dark chocolate, or I'm traveling and can't access this type of food. Or I just feel like going out to a fabulous restaurant and trying something new and decadent on the menu. That 20 percent "wiggle room" helps me to not feel guilty when I'm not on track with my eating. In fact, I can enjoy my little moments of not being "on the path" because I know that I'm on it 80 percent of the time.

For me this approach to nutrition works. It's manageable, it's sustainable, and it makes me feel amazing. It's a lifestyle! No longer do I struggle with my weight. My long plague of digestive issues (bloating and acid burn) is over, and at the age of fifty-three I have off-the-charts energy that enables me to do the things I love to do, and to keep up with my eleven-, thirteen-, and nineteen-year-old kids. This approach also gives me room to be human and to enjoy my life to the fullest.

Next time you eat, take a look at your plate. If your plate does not have 80 percent plant-based foods, 10 percent protein, 10 percent complex carbs, and a dose of healthy fats, why not change it? Try the 80-10-10 rule for twenty-one days and see if you feel a difference in your

body, mind, and soul. We have such an abundance of super, high-vitality foods from our soil; let's start eating a more plant-based diet. Not only is it good for you, it's good for the farmers and for the planet!

All the recipes that I share with you in this book are based on the 80-10-10 rule, and there is even a 20 percent totally decadent sweet-treat section for you—because that's OK too! We have to live fit, but we also have to live life too.

All I ask is that you honor your body as the Temple of the Divine that it is. My first yoga teacher, Yogi Amrit Desai, taught:

> *In search of the divine we go everywhere. We go to places of pilgrimage, visit temples, follow many paths and disciplines—and ignore our bodies. Your body is the most sacred place of pilgrimage you'll ever come to. It is the dwelling place of the divine spirit, it is the temple of God. Go within and experience the glory of God within you.*
>
> —Yogi Amrit Desai

Let your food be an offering to your temple. Let it fill you with prana, with life force, and with a whole lot of love. May you always be grateful to Mother Earth for providing it, the farmers who grew it, and the hands that prepared it.

Namaste.

# How to Use This Book

There are over one hundred recipes in this cookbook, divided into seven sections. Breakfast Time shares green power smoothies and breakfast ideas to kick-start your day. In Main Meal or Lunchtime, you'll find salads, mains, and sides that will supercharge your life. Everyone loves snacks, and the Snack Time section's gluten-free, vegan, superfood recipes will rock your world. In the Dinnertime section, I show you how to prepare healing, high-vitality soups that are filling and nutritious. Discover nut milks, nut butters, salad dressings, and other goodies to have on hand in your pantry in All the Time, and in Teatime, dive into healing teas, lattes, and elixirs. Lastly, I give you delicious recipes for the 20 Percent time: sweet treats! I adore these recipes, many of which came from family and friends.

I organized the book this way as this is how I eat and plan my meals. You can select recipes from any section, using the 80-10-10 rule. For example, you may want to have a breakfast frittata for lunch or have Live Fit Detox Bars for an afternoon snack. There are no hard and fast rules for you to follow. This is my gift to you: simply delicious recipes for living fit, living life, and living love that you and your family can enjoy.

This cookbook is just the beginning of your journey of transformation. When you start feeling good in your body, it translates into every area of your life. Please, take a walk on the wild side with me. Be willing to let go of the things, habits, places, and people that no longer serve you. Treat your body like a Temple of the Divine and please, get in your kitchen and begin to change the way you and your family eat, one day at a time. Don't strive for perfection. Just make little changes every day. Love yourself, love your body, love your life, and give thanks for every single moment that has led you to this one, reading this book, hearing these words right now.

I can't wait to take you on this never-ending journey of discovery. Take a deep breath in, and a long breath out, and be here now. Read through the pages and find one recipe or nugget of wisdom that you can try today. Little changes add up to a lot. Soon you will be living fit, living life, and living love too and encouraging those around you to do the same.

# WHAT A HIGH-VITALITY PANTRY LOOKS LIKE

Here is a list of the basic items that I always have in my pantry for high-vitality cooking. Most of these items can be found in the supermarket or your local health-food store. I've not included veggies, fruits, or fresh produce here, as those items should be bought as fresh as possible. I also encourage you to buy local and avoid imported foods. You want to eat as close to the source as possible.

As much as you can, avoid processed foods. My rule is: don't eat anything that comes out of a bag, a can, or a box and has more than one ingredient. All foods are 'processed' to some extent. You pick an apple from the tree or you juice a lemon, and that is technically 'processing.' However, I'm referring to foods that are chemically processed—foods that have sugar, salt, preservatives, or unhealthy fats added to them. Additionally, most of the carbohydrates in processed foods are 'simple' carbohydrates that spike blood sugar levels and produce other unwanted effects. Finally, preparing your meals from fresh foods allows you to control what goes into each dish. If you or someone you cook for has any food allergies or ingredients they want or need to avoid, cooking fresh meals rather than reaching for a box means no unintended allergic reactions.

Always look at the menu you're planning for the week before you go shopping, and commit to buying only what you need. This way, you can avoid impulse buys, which are often less healthy and can lead to food waste.

### OILS

- [ ] Avocado oil
- [ ] Cold-pressed coconut oil
- [ ] High-quality extra-virgin olive oil
- [ ] High-quality sesame oil

### NUTS & SEEDS

- [ ] Cashew nuts
- [ ] Chia seeds
- [ ] Flaxseeds
- [ ] Hemp seeds
- [ ] Pine nuts
- [ ] Pumpkin seeds
- [ ] Sesame seeds (black and white)
- [ ] Sliced almonds
- [ ] Sunflower seeds
- [ ] Walnuts
- [ ] Whole raw almonds

### FLOURS & GRAINS

- [ ] Almond flour
- [ ] Almond meal
- [ ] Black rice
- [ ] Brown rice noodles
- [ ] Bulgur wheat
- [ ] Flaxseed meal
- [ ] Gluten-free flour
- [ ] Gluten-free old-fashioned oats
- [ ] Gluten-free steel-cut oats
- [ ] Millet
- [ ] Nutritional yeast
- [ ] Quinoa
- [ ] Short-grain brown rice
- [ ] Whole-grain pasta

## LEGUMES

- [ ] Canned black beans
- [ ] Canned black-eyed peas
- [ ] Canned chickpeas
- [ ] Dried black beans
- [ ] Dried black-eyed peas
- [ ] Dried chickpeas
- [ ] Gungo peas (aka pigeon peas)
- [ ] Lentils
- [ ] Mung beans

## DRIED FRUITS

- [ ] Blueberries
- [ ] Figs
- [ ] Goji berries
- [ ] Golden berries
- [ ] Mulberries
- [ ] Organic dried cranberries (using organic dried is ideal, but they are expensive and difficult to find; when in doubt use what's available)
- [ ] Pitted dates

## POWDERS & SUPPLEMENTS

- [ ] Maca powder (available from most health-food stores or Amazon.com)
- [ ] Moringa powder (available from most health-food stores or Amazon.com)
- [ ] Spirulina (available from most health-food stores or Amazon.com)

## VINEGARS & SEASONINGS

- [ ] Aged balsamic vinegar
- [ ] Apple cider vinegar
- [ ] Bay leaves
- [ ] Cayenne pepper
- [ ] Chili powder
- [ ] Dijon mustard
- [ ] Dried mint
- [ ] Dried thyme
- [ ] Fish sauce
- [ ] Garlic powder
- [ ] Ground black pepper
- [ ] Ground coriander
- [ ] Ground cumin
- [ ] Himalayan sea salt
- [ ] Indian curry powder
- [ ] Jerk seasoning
- [ ] Organic cinnamon powder
- [ ] Pimento berries (allspice)
- [ ] Rice wine vinegar
- [ ] Scotch bonnet sauce
- [ ] Smoked paprika
- [ ] Thai green curry paste
- [ ] Thai red curry sauce
- [ ] Wheat-free tamari

## OTHER

- [ ] Baking powder
- [ ] Baking soda
- [ ] Canned unsweetened coconut milk
- [ ] Chocolate chips
- [ ] Coconut nectar (great low-glycemic sweetener that has a nearly neutral pH)
- [ ] Dry coconut
- [ ] Ground cardamom
- [ ] Ground cloves
- [ ] Ground ginger (in case you can't find fresh)
- [ ] Ground turmeric (in case you can't find fresh)
- [ ] Honey
- [ ] Matcha tea
- [ ] Olives (black and Nicoise)
- [ ] Organic brown sugar
- [ ] Organic coffee
- [ ] Organic low-sodium chicken broth
- [ ] Organic maple syrup
- [ ] Pomegranate molasses
- [ ] Pumpkin
- [ ] Pure vanilla extract (not vanilla flavoring, which is made from synthetic ingredients)
- [ ] Raw cacao nibs
- [ ] Raw cacao powder (it's best to use raw cacao, as processing may incorporate chemicals)
- [ ] Rice wraps
- [ ] Scotch bonnet pepper
- [ ] Tahini
- [ ] Unsweetened shredded coconut
- [ ] Yam, sweet potato, yellow yam

# EQUIPMENT LIST

Apart from obvious kitchen needs like great pots and pans (cast-iron is best, because it can stand high heat and it's nonstick), sharp knives, and cutting boards, there are a few items I consistently rely on. Here are some of the tools that make life easier in the kitchen. The most expensive thing on this list and the one I absolutely can't do without is my Vitamix. I use it all day, every day. Any good high-speed blender will do, but my Vitamix just goes and goes.

- [ ] Baking sheets
- [ ] Box grater
- [ ] Coconut opener
- [ ] Food processor
- [ ] Glass measuring cups
- [ ] Glass storage containers in various sizes
- [ ] Handheld electric mixer
- [ ] Hinged citrus press
- [ ] Mandoline
- [ ] Mason jars
- [ ] Measuring spoons
- [ ] Metal spatula
- [ ] Nesting stainless steel bowls of various sizes

- [ ] Nut-milk bags
- [ ] Parchment paper
- [ ] Rubber or silicone spatulas
- [ ] Small prep bowls
- [ ] Soup ladle
- [ ] Spiralizer or spiral slicer
- [ ] Tall soup pot
- [ ] Tongs
- [ ] Vegetable peeler
- [ ] Vitamix or high-speed blender
- [ ] Wax paper
- [ ] Wooden spoons

Protein Power Kale and Mushroom Frittata, page 48

# Breakfast Time

*Green Power Smoothies and Breakfast*
*Ideas to Kick-Start Your Day*

Before my detox journey, breakfast time was always a challenge for me. I knew it was important, but I was usually rushing out the door in the morning, grabbing a large cup of coffee (loaded with milk and sugar) and a store-bought granola bar on my way out. By eleven o'clock I was starving, reaching for another cup of coffee, and then having a huge and probably not-so-healthy lunch. When I was introduced to green smoothies and started making my own homemade protein bars and granola cereal, I really felt a difference. By having an alkalizing green smoothie first thing in the morning, I not only get an instant boost of energy, but I'm also loading up on easily digestible vital vitamins, minerals, fiber, and phytonutrients. Having my homemade bars means I always have a filling superfood snack ready to go. If I've worked out hard in the gym, I add a couple boiled eggs for a little extra protein. To save time, I make my bars and granola on the weekends and prep my smoothies each night; I'm still rushing out the door in the morning, but now I have my healthy breakfast routine down and no longer get those hangry (hungry + angry) midmorning pangs!

Mango Tango Green Smoothie, page 25

## GET YOUR GREEN SHAKE!

Nothing makes me feel better than starting my day with a green shake. Not only are they the most efficient way to get all my phytonutrients, vitamins, minerals, and fiber, but green smoothies also help to alkalize the body and provide energy all day. In order for your body to function optimally, you need to be in an alkaline state. Over time, regularly eating a diet high in acid-forming foods may increase the risk for chronic diseases. A high-speed blender is vital to creating a smooth shake that's easy to drink. For my shakes, I usually use the water from one young jelly coconut or Homemade Vanilla Almond Milk (page 158) as a base and always add a teaspoon of my favorite superfoods: maca powder, spirulina, and Moringa powder. If you don't have the fruits and greens on hand that a recipe calls for, feel free to make your own substitutions. Here are some of the vegetables, fruits, and add-ons I use. Please note that I use only one serving of fruit per smoothie. While fruits are full of fiber and so good for you, they contain lots of sugar, so focus more on the greens than the fruits to keep the body alkaline. Just make sure the ingredients are as fresh, organic, and as local as possible. And if you're not sure it's clean, please wash and rewash your produce!

### Veggies

Bok choy, callaloo (a Caribbean plant similar to spinach), spinach, kale, mustard greens, mixed lettuces, cabbage, parsley, cilantro, beets, carrots, avocado, cucumber, zucchini, celery, and aloe

### Fruits

Coconut, pineapple, mango, papaya, berries of all kinds, melon, apples, dates, bananas, and watermelon

### Superfood Add-Ons

Ginger, turmeric, Moringa powder, spirulina powder, flaxseeds, hemp seeds, chia seeds, vanilla extract, organic cinnamon powder, maca powder, and raw cacao powder

# Pineapple-Ginger Moringa Smoothie

This is hands down my go-to shake. Made with sweet pineapple and ginger to aid digestion and combat inflammation, plus superfood Moringa powder that's rich in vitamins, minerals, calcium, and protein, this is the recipe I recommend to green-shake newbies because it's easy to make and everyone loves it.

| YIELD: 2 cups | PREP TIME: 3 to 5 minutes |
|---|---|

## PROCEDURE

1. Blend all ingredients together in a high-speed blender.

2. Serve and enjoy!

## INGREDIENTS

2 medium slices pineapple

½ cup greens (kale, bok choy, spinach, or any greens you have on hand)

½ medium cucumber, quartered

1 stalk celery, cut in thirds

1 medium carrot, cut in thirds

1 (3-inch) knob fresh ginger, peeled

1 teaspoon Moringa powder

1 teaspoon flaxseeds or chia seeds

1¼ cups coconut water

1 teaspoon honey or 2 pitted dates

1 handful ice

# Mango Tango Green Smoothie

OK, seriously, mango season is the best time of the year! You can make this delicious shake long after mango season is over by dicing and freezing your mangoes. In fact, don't waste your produce: cut up and freeze any fruit while it's in season so that you have it on hand when you're feeling rushed in the morning; this way you don't have to add ice.

---

YIELD: 2 cups                    PREP TIME: 3 to 5 minutes

---

## PROCEDURE

1.  Blend all ingredients together in a high-speed blender.

2.  Serve and enjoy!

## INGREDIENTS

1 large ripe mango, diced

½ cup greens (kale, bok choy, spinach, or any greens you have on hand)

½ medium cucumber, halved

1 stalk celery, cut in thirds

1 teaspoon flaxseeds or chia seeds

1 pinch cinnamon

1 cup coconut water

½ cup Homemade Vanilla Almond Milk (page 158) or store-bought unsweetened almond milk

½ teaspoon vanilla extract

1 handful ice

# Banana Cacao Rama Smoothie

If a green smoothie isn't cutting it, and I'm craving something creamier and more filling, this shake is it! The banana, almond butter, and raw chocolate combo is out of this world.

---

YIELD: 2 cups                    PREP TIME: 3 to 5 minutes

---

## PROCEDURE

1. Blend all ingredients together in a high-speed blender.

2. Serve and enjoy!

## INGREDIENTS

1 large ripe banana

½ cup greens (kale, bok choy, spinach, or any greens you have on hand)

1 tablespoon raw cacao powder

1 teaspoon flaxseeds or chia seeds

¼ teaspoon cinnamon

1 cup coconut water

½ cup Homemade Vanilla Almond Milk (page 158), Homemade Coconut Milk (page 159), or store-bought unsweetened almond or coconut milk

2 tablespoons Homemade Sweet Cinnamon Almond Butter (page 161), or store-bought almond butter

½ teaspoon vanilla extract

1 teaspoon honey or 2 pitted dates

1 handful ice

# Maca Machine Smoothie

At the Body Shop, the amazing little gym in Montego Bay where I work out, my nickname is Maca. Maca, along with spirulina and Moringa powder, is one of the superfoods I eat every day. Grown in the Andes Mountains, maca's benefits include hormone balancing, increased energy, improved sexual function, sharper memory, and stronger focus. Try this smoothie before you reach for something unhealthy in the morning. The sweet and satisfying combo of raw cacao, maca powder, and banana sure does the trick—plus you're still getting your greens. Bring on the maca, baby!

---

YIELD: 2 cups　　　　　　PREP TIME: 3 to 5 minutes

---

## PROCEDURE

1. Blend all ingredients together in a high-speed blender.

2. Serve and enjoy!

## INGREDIENTS

1 large ripe banana

1 cup greens (kale, bok choy, spinach, or whatever greens you have on hand)

2 teaspoons raw cacao powder

1 teaspoon maca powder

¼ teaspoon cinnamon

1 cup Homemade Vanilla Almond Milk (page 158), Homemade Coconut Milk (page 159), or store-bought unsweetened almond or coconut milk

1 cup coconut water

1 teaspoon honey or 2 pitted dates

¼ teaspoon vanilla extract

1 handful ice

Shakti Granola Bars Three Ways, page 53

# Berry Delicious Antioxidant Smoothie

When I'm in Jamaica, I try not to buy imported fruits and vegetables. I prefer to get my food from as close to its source as possible. However, when I'm away and can find organic berries such as blueberries, blackberries, and raspberries, I'm all over it! This is my very berry best shake to make when I'm traveling. If you can't get fresh berries, the frozen ones are fine—just make sure they're organic.

---

**YIELD:** 2 cups          **PREP TIME:** 3 to 5 minutes

---

## PROCEDURE

1. Blend all ingredients together in a high-speed blender.

2. Serve and enjoy!

## INGREDIENTS

1 cup berries (your favorite or a combo!)

½ cup red cabbage (or kale, bok choy, spinach, or whatever greens you have on hand)

1 tablespoon coconut oil

1 teaspoon flaxseeds or chia seeds

1 cup coconut water

1 cup Homemade Vanilla Almond Milk (page 158), Homemade Coconut Milk (page 159), or store-bought unsweetened almond milk

1 teaspoon honey or 2 pitted dates

1 handful ice

# Can't Beet It Smoothie

This shake is not only delicious, but it's also good for your heart! Beets improve athletic performance, lower blood pressure, and increase blood flow. You can't beet this recipe for a Life Fit life!

---

YIELD: 2 cups          PREP TIME: 3 to 5 minutes

---

## PROCEDURE

1. Blend all ingredients together in a high-speed blender.

2. Serve and enjoy

## INGREDIENTS

1 medium beet, peeled and chopped

1 carrot, chopped

1 apple, diced (or any fruit you love; papaya and pineapple work well here too)

½ cup fresh parsley

1 (3-inch) knob ginger

1 cup coconut water

1 teaspoon honey or 2 pitted dates

1 handful ice

Homemade Vanilla Almond Milk, page 158

# Creamy Papaya-Turmeric Smoothie

Papayas are abundant in Jamaica and so, so sweet. This anti-inflammatory, creamy, and oh-so-healing smoothie is good for your digestion. Papayas contain powerful digestive enzymes, and turmeric contains soothing chemicals that reduce inflammation; this is an amazing recipe if you suffer from IBS, bloating, or indigestion.

| YIELD: 2 cups | PREP TIME: 3 to 5 minutes |
| --- | --- |

## PROCEDURE

1. Blend all ingredients together in a high-speed blender.

2. Serve and enjoy!

## INGREDIENTS

1 cup ripe papaya, diced

¼ cup greens (kale, bok choy, spinach, or whatever greens you have on hand)

1 (2-inch) knob fresh turmeric, or 1 teaspoon ground

1 (3-inch) knob fresh ginger, peeled

1 tablespoon coconut oil

1 teaspoon flaxseeds or chia seeds

2 cups coconut water

½ cup Homemade Vanilla Almond Milk (page 158), Homemade Coconut Milk (page 159), or store-bought unsweetened almond or coconut milk

2 teaspoons honey or 4 pitted dates

½ teaspoon vanilla extract

1 handful ice

# Vanilla, Coconut, and Chia Seed Pudding

This became my new breakfast obsession after I discovered it during a yoga retreat in Bali. Packed with protein, incredible amounts of fiber, omega-3s, antioxidants, potassium, magnesium, and calcium, chia seeds boost energy like nothing else, improve endurance, and are fantastic for digestion, especially if you have a sluggish colon. This recipe is delicious for breakfast as well as dessert. Add your favorite fruits and/or nuts as toppings. Here is my favorite chia seed breakfast recipe so far!

---

YIELD: 2 cups          PREP TIME: 10 to 15 minutes + at least 4 hours in fridge

---

## PROCEDURE

1. Pour almond milk, chia seeds, shredded coconut, raw cacao nibs, honey, vanilla, and cinnamon into a high-speed blender and blend at a slow speed for 20 seconds, or until smooth.

2. Pour into 2 (8-ounce) or 1 (16-ounce) glass jar. Refrigerate overnight or at least 4 hours, until the chia seeds absorb all the liquid.

3. Remove from fridge and top with fruit and nuts of your choice.

4. Stir everything together and enjoy!

5. The pudding will keep 3 to 4 days in the fridge.

## INGREDIENTS

1½ cups Homemade Vanilla Almond Milk (page 158) or store-bought unsweetened almond milk

⅓ cup chia seeds

1 tablespoon unsweetened shredded coconut

2 tablespoons raw cacao nibs

1 tablespoon honey or maple syrup

1 teaspoon vanilla extract

¼ teaspoon cinnamon

Fruits and nuts of your choice

# Gluten-Free Steel-Cut Overnight Oats with Toasted Walnuts, Coconut, and Berries

Sometimes I really want something warm and soothing in my tummy in the morning. Now I eat gluten-free steel-cut oats, which are much less processed and have loads more fiber than old-fashioned oats. They do take a little longer to cook, so I make them the night before and put them in the fridge. The next morning all I need to do is warm them up, top with fruit and nuts, and I'm ready to go!

---

YIELD: 2½ cups     PREP TIME: 10 to 15 minutes     COOK TIME: 10 minutes

---

## PROCEDURE

1. Bring the water to a boil. Add the oats, cover, and simmer for 5 to 8 minutes.

2. Add the flaxseeds, chia seeds, cinnamon, and nutmeg, stirring continuously for 1 to 2 minutes.

3. Add the milk and honey and remove from the heat.

4. Cool, then pour into 2 (10-ounce) containers and top each with coconut and walnuts. Store overnight in the fridge.

5. Add your mixed berries in the morning!

6. This can be enjoyed warm or straight from the fridge if you are in a rush.

## INGREDIENTS

2 cups water

½ cup gluten-free steel-cut oats

1 tablespoon ground flaxseeds

1 tablespoon chia seeds

¼ teaspoon cinnamon

¼ teaspoon ground nutmeg

½ cup Homemade Vanilla Almond Milk (page 158), Homemade Coconut Milk (page 159), or store-bought unsweetened almond or coconut milk

1 tablespoon honey

2 teaspoons unsweetened shredded coconut, toasted

2 teaspoons chopped walnuts

2 ounces mixed berries or fruit of your choice

# Groovy Granola Cereal

OK, I'm the first to tell you I am a hippy chick. Anything called granola gets my groove on. Unfortunately, there are now tons of very unhealthy granola cereals and granola bars on the market, and that's why I make my own. This crunchy, sweet-and-salty mix of roasted gluten-free oats, dried fruit, nuts, seeds, and shaved coconut will have you disco dancing all day! Try it with my Homemade Vanilla Almond Milk (page 158) or Homemade Coconut Milk (page 159), topped with fresh fruit. It's perfect for breakfast or as a postworkout snack. Your temple will love you!

| YIELD: 8 cups | PREP TIME: 30 minutes | COOK TIME: 30 minutes |
| --- | --- | --- |

## PROCEDURE

1. Preheat the oven to 350°F.

2. Mix all ingredients except cranberries together in a large bowl and spread on a large baking sheet.

3. Toast in the oven for 25 to 30 minutes, stirring occasionally, until golden brown.

4. Remove from oven, stir the cranberries into the mixture, and let cool.

5. Store in an airtight container in a cool, dry place up to a month—if it lasts that long!

## INGREDIENTS

5 cups gluten-free old-fashioned oats

1 cup unsweetened shredded coconut

½ cup pumpkin seeds

½ cup sliced almonds

½ cup whole almonds

½ cup flaxseeds

½ cup sunflower seeds

½ cup maple syrup

1 tablespoon coconut oil

1 teaspoon cinnamon

1 teaspoon vanilla extract

¼ teaspoon Himalayan sea salt

½ cup dried cranberries

# Gluten-Free Breakfast Banana Bread with Raw Cacao Nibs or Chocolate Chips

Don't know what to do with your over-ripe bananas? Make banana bread! Here's a recipe that Miss Neng and I worked on for over a year, and I think we finally got it. Made with gluten-free flour, this rich and satisfying bread contains hemp and flaxseeds for added protein and omega-3s for heart health. You can replace the raw cacao nibs with chocolate chips if you wish for the kids. Try this with my Homemade Sweet Cinnamon Almond Butter (page 161) for the best breakfast ever.

| YIELD: 1 loaf | PREP TIME: 15 minutes | COOK TIME: 60 minutes |
| --- | --- | --- |

## PROCEDURE

1. Preheat the oven to 350°F and grease a 9-by-5-inch loaf pan with the two tablespoons butter.

2. Using an electric mixer, cream together the remaining butter and the brown sugar until well combined.

3. Add the eggs and mashed bananas to the butter mixture and combine well.

4. In a separate bowl, sift together the flour, baking powder, baking soda, and salt. Add the flaxseeds and hemp seeds to the flour mixture and stir to combine.

5. Add the dry ingredients, the cacao nibs, and the vanilla to the butter mixture, and mix on medium speed for 3 to 5 minutes, until thoroughly combined.

6. Pour the batter into the prepared pan.

7. Arrange the banana slices on the top for decoration.

8. Bake for 50 to 60 minutes, until a skewer or toothpick inserted in the middle of the loaf comes out clean.

## INGREDIENTS

2 tablespoons plus ½ cup butter, divided

½ cup brown sugar

2 large eggs

4 ripe bananas, mashed smooth

½ cup gluten-free flour

1 teaspoon baking powder

1 teaspoon baking soda

½ teaspoon salt

½ cup ground flaxseeds

¼ cup hemp seeds

⅓ cup raw cacao nibs or chocolate chips

1 teaspoon vanilla extract

1 ripe banana, sliced

## CREAMING

First, soften the butter. Do this by placing the butter on the counter until it reaches cool room temperature. Do not allow it to start melting. Then, cut the butter into approximately ½-inch cubes and transfer them to a large mixing bowl. Starting on low speed, beat the butter with an electric mixer until it looks creamy. This should take about 30 seconds. Turn the speed of the mixer to medium. Beat the butter for 1 to 2 minutes, stopping the mixer every so often to scrape the sides of the bowl with a rubber spatula, and to scrape any butter that is caught in the beaters. With the mixer on low speed, gradually add the sugar. Increase the speed to medium. Again, stop the mixer every so often to scrape the sides of the bowl with a rubber spatula, and to wipe off any of the mixture that is caught in the beaters. Continue mixing until the mixture has almost doubled in mass and has lightened to a whiteish-yellow color. Small ridges will form in the wake of the mixture once it reaches this texture, or the texture of your spoon or spatula will remain after you stir. This takes up to 5 minutes.

# Plantain, Smashed Avocado, and Poached Egg Breakfast Pizza

I love both ripe and green plantains for this recipe, but somehow the green plantain works better for me with the avocado and eggs. Try it with both and see what works best for you. You can make the crust ahead and freeze it so it's easy to pop in the oven in the morning. Get creative! This pizza is not just for breakfast. Top yours with hummus or Jerked Almond Pâté (page 126), or make it into a wonderful gluten-free pizza base for other meals. It's so amazing.

| YIELD: 4 personal-sized pizzas | PREP TIME: 30 minutes | COOK TIME: 25 minutes |
|---|---|---|

## PROCEDURE

1. Preheat the oven to 450°F.

2. Heat a large sauté pan over medium heat for 2 to 3 minutes. Add the coconut oil and swirl to evenly coat the pan.

3. Pan-fry the plantains for 6 minutes, until soft and golden.

4. Transfer the cooked plantains to a food processor or high-speed blender and pulse until a little crumbly.

5. Add the water and olive oil and pulse again until you get a doughy consistency.

6. Add the coconut flour, garlic powder, thyme, and ¼ teaspoon of the sea salt and pulse again until well combined and a smooth dough has formed.

7. Remove the dough from the food processor and divide it into four even portions.

8. Press each portion of dough evenly onto a baking sheet or pizza pan (see note) in the shape of a circle, wetting your hands if the dough starts to stick. Crust should be ¼ inch thick.

9. Bake for 20 to 25 minutes, until edges are lightly brown and crisp.

## INGREDIENTS

2 tablespoons coconut oil

3 large green plantains, peeled and chopped

1 cup water

2 tablespoons extra-virgin olive oil

1½ tablespoons coconut flour

½ teaspoon garlic powder

1 teaspoon fresh thyme, chopped

½ teaspoon Himalayan sea salt, divided

2 large eggs

1 large avocado

¼ teaspoon ground black pepper

10. While the crusts are baking, poach or hard-boil the eggs and smash the avocado with the remaining sea salt and the black pepper.

11. Remove the crusts from the oven, smother each one with one-quarter of the smashed avocado and top with half of a poached or hard-boiled egg. Season with more salt and pepper if you choose.

**NOTE:** For the best browning, use a nonstick 12-inch pizza pan and make sure it's gray, not black. Black versions can burn the dough.

Plantain, Smashed Avocado, and Poached Egg Breakfast Pizza, page 44

### EASY POACHED EGGS

1. Crack an egg into a small bowl or onto a saucer.

2. Bring a pan of water filled at least 2 inches deep to a simmer.

3. Tip the egg into the pan.

4. Cook for 2 minutes, turn off the heat, and leave the pan for 8 to 10 minutes, until the egg white has set.

5. Lift the egg out with a slotted spoon and drain it on paper towels.

# Protein Power Kale and Mushroom Frittata

This recipe is a Sunday morning special in our house. You can use any greens you have on hand, but the mushrooms are what really make it so yummy. I like to use shiitake or oyster mushrooms, but any type works here. Light and filling and packed with nutrition, it's a great postworkout protein-packed meal for breakfast, lunch, or dinner.

| YIELD: 2 servings | PREP TIME: 10 minutes | COOK TIME: 15 minutes |
| --- | --- | --- |

## PROCEDURE

1. Put the eggs, egg whites, sea salt, and pepper in a medium bowl. Whisk together and set aside.

2. Heat a medium sauté pan over medium heat for 2 to 3 minutes. Add the olive oil and swirl to evenly coat the pan. Sauté the kale, onions, peppers, mushrooms, nutritional yeast, and thyme for 2 to 3 minutes, until the vegetables have softened.

3. Add the egg mixture to the vegetables, place the sliced tomatoes on top, and cook until the mixture is firm (about 8 minutes). Using a wide spatula, flip the frittata.

4. Cook for another minute, or until golden brown.

5. Top with Parmesan cheese (optional). Serve nice and hot!

## INGREDIENTS

3 large eggs

2 large egg whites

Pinch Himalayan sea salt

Pinch ground black pepper

1 tablespoon extra-virgin olive oil

1 cup chopped kale (or any greens you love)

1 small onion, chopped

1 small yellow or red bell pepper, sliced

3 ounces fresh shiitake, oyster, or button mushrooms, sliced

1 teaspoon nutritional yeast

1 teaspoon chopped fresh thyme, or ½ teaspoon dried

1 small tomato, sliced

¼ cup shredded Parmesan cheese (optional)

# Hemp Protein Chocolate Bars

I love these bars for a midmorning snack topped with a little Homemade Sweet Cinnamon Almond Butter (page 161) or with my afternoon Glorious Golden Milk (page 192). Not only is hemp protein a perfect balance of omega-3 and omega-6 fatty acids that promote heart health, but it's also high in GLA (gamma-linolenic acid), which is proven to naturally balance hormones. I'm all for that.

| YIELD: 24 bars | PREP TIME: 20 minutes | COOK TIME: 40 minutes |
| --- | --- | --- |

## PROCEDURE

1. Preheat the oven to 350°F.

2. In a medium bowl, stir together the oats, flaxseeds, walnuts, almond meal, raw cacao nibs, coconut, hemp seeds, chia seeds, sesame seeds, raw cacao powder, and cinnamon.

3. Blend the dates with the water, coconut oil, vanilla, and honey in a food processor or high-speed blender till smooth.

4. In a large bowl, combine the dry and wet ingredients and stir till evenly mixed.

5. Spread the mixture in a 9-by-13-inch nonstick baking pan. Cut into 24 small squares.

6. Bake for 30 to 40 minutes, until crispy.

7. Store bars in an airtight glass container for up to 1 week, or freeze for 2 to 3 months.

## INGREDIENTS

1 cup gluten-free old-fashioned oats

½ cup ground flaxseeds

½ cup chopped walnuts

¼ cup almond meal

¼ cup raw cacao nibs

¼ cup unsweetened shredded coconut

¼ cup hemp seeds

¼ cup chia seeds

¼ cup sesame seeds, toasted

2 tablespoons raw cacao powder

½ teaspoon cinnamon

1 cup pitted dates

1 cup water

2 tablespoons coconut oil

1 teaspoon vanilla extract

2 tablespoons honey

# Live Fit Detox Bars

If you want to live fit, you need to have ready-to-go snacks that are not only filling but also deliver great nutrition. These bars are it! They are high in fiber and omega-3 fatty acids, plus they're easy to make and easy to carry. You're going to love them.

| YIELD: 24 bars | PREP TIME: 15 minutes | COOK TIME: 25 minutes |
| --- | --- | --- |

## PROCEDURE

1. Preheat the oven to 350°F.

2. Combine the oats, walnuts, and coconut in the bowl of a food processor and pulse until finely ground.

3. Transfer the oat/walnut/coconut mixture to a large bowl and add all of the remaining ingredients, mixing well with your hands.

4. Pour the mixture into a 9-by-13-inch nonstick baking pan, pressing down till evenly distributed. Slice into 24 bars.

5. Bake for 25 minutes, or until golden brown.

6. Cool completely.

7. Remove the bars from the pan carefully and store in an airtight glass container for up to 1 week, or freeze for 2 to 3 months.

## INGREDIENTS

2 cups gluten-free old-fashioned oats

½ cup raw walnuts

¼ cup unsweetened shredded coconut

⅓ cup flaxseeds (ground)

¼ cup sliced raw almonds

¼ cup whole raw almonds

¼ cup pumpkin seeds

½ teaspoon cinnamon

½ teaspoon Himalayan sea salt

¼ teaspoon ground cloves

¼ teaspoon ground cardamom

¼ cup extra-virgin olive oil or coconut oil

¼ cup coconut nectar or honey

# Shakti Granola Bars Three Ways

When I was pregnant with Toby, my eldest daughter, I craved something sweet and crunchy. I wanted it to be healthy, and so the Shakti Granola Bars were born. These were my very first bars! Soon I began selling them at the gym I owned at the time, Shakti Mind Body Fitness. I swear there were some people who came to the gym only to eat the bars. If you don't want to use chocolate, substitute the same amount of dates or cranberries. Shakti means the life force within you; be ready to increase your life force when you eat these blessed bars.

| YIELD: 24 bars | PREP TIME: 15 minutes | COOK TIME: 50 minutes |
| --- | --- | --- |

## PROCEDURE

1. Preheat the oven to 350°F.

2. In a large bowl, combine the oats, flour, flaxseeds, brown sugar, chocolate chips, and cinnamon.

3. Add the apple juice, olive oil, and vanilla and stir to combine.

4. Pour the mixture into a 9-by-13-inch nonstick baking pan, pressing down till evenly distributed. Slice into 24 bars.

5. Sprinkle the sesame seeds evenly over the top of the bars.

6. Bake for 40 to 50 minutes, or until golden brown and crispy.

7. Cool completely.

8. Remove the bars from the pan carefully and store in an airtight container for up to 1 week, or freeze for 2 to 3 months.

## INGREDIENTS

2½ cups gluten-free old-fashioned oats

1 cup gluten-free flour or whole wheat flour

¼ cup ground flaxseeds

¼ cup brown sugar

¼ cup chocolate chips

½ teaspoon cinnamon

1 cup apple juice

¼ cup extra-virgin olive oil

1 teaspoon vanilla extract

1 tablespoon sesame seeds

Shakti Granola Bars Three Ways, page 53, and Glorious Golden Milk, page 192

# Almond Bliss Balls

When I first started making my own almond milk, I threw away the almond pulp. But one day my beautiful friend Dr. Tracey Wright showed me what a wonderful ingredient it is for making gluten-free raw crackers, cookies, breads, etc. That's how I started making Almond Bliss Balls. Whether you eat them raw or baked, get creative with whatever fruit, nuts, and seeds you have on hand and make your own version. I grab a couple when I'm on the go for a perfect superfood snack.

YIELD: 24 balls          PREP TIME: 20 minutes

## PROCEDURE

1. In a large bowl, mix all the ingredients together until well combined.

2. Roll into walnut-size balls.

3. Freeze the balls in an airtight container.

4. Thaw and eat them raw or pop them (frozen) in a toaster oven for 10 to 15 minutes.

## INGREDIENTS

2 cups almond pulp (see Homemade Vanilla Almond Milk recipe, page 158)

¼ cup unsweetened shredded coconut, toasted

¼ cup chopped pitted dates or figs

¼ cup chopped walnuts or almonds

¼ cup raw cacao nibs

2 tablespoons flaxseeds

½ teaspoon cinnamon

2 tablespoons Homemade Sweet Cinnamon Almond Butter (page 161)

2 tablespoons honey

1 teaspoon vanilla extract

# Sunflower Seed–Cranberry Superfood Balls

These little superfood balls are slightly sweet—they'll satisfy your sweet tooth for sure—but have a whole lot of goodness and will keep you surprisingly full for hours. I like to take them with me when I'm traveling; they're easy to carry and keep me going when I don't have time to stop and eat.

**YIELD:** 24 balls          **PREP TIME:** 70 to 80 minutes

## PROCEDURE

1. In a large bowl, mix all the ingredients together until well combined. If the mixture is too dry to hold together in a ball, add more honey or maple syrup. If it's too wet to hold together in a ball, add more ground flaxseeds or sunflower seeds.

2. Place the mixture in the fridge for at least an hour, until mixture is chilled throughout, then remove and roll into 1-inch balls.

3. Store leftovers (if there are any!) in the fridge in an airtight container for up to 7 days.

## INGREDIENTS

1 cup gluten-free old-fashioned oats

½ cup Homemade Sweet Cinnamon Almond Butter (page 161) or store-bought almond butter

½ cup ground flaxseeds, plus more as needed

½ cup shredded unsweetened coconut, toasted

4 tablespoons sunflower seeds

2 tablespoons dried cranberries

2 tablespoons sliced almonds, plus more as needed

⅓ cup maple syrup or honey, plus more as needed

1½ teaspoons vanilla extract

Spicy Mahi-Mahi Fish Burgers, page 98, and Daikon and Carrot Salad, page 76

# Main Meal or Lunchtime

*Salads, Mains, and Sides*
*That Will Supercharge Your Life!*

Lunch is usually the biggest meal of my day. Midday is when your digestive fires are burning bright and your body can readily convert food into precious energy. In this section you'll find my absolute favorite recipes. These are the meals I use for my Live Fit Detox Programs, but also what you would probably eat if you came to my home for lunch. Most of the recipes are plant-based, as I find that making my main meal vegetarian helps me stick to my rule of eating plant-based foods 80 percent of the time. Weekends are a great time to cook your beans, prep your salads and healthy carbs, and stock your freezer with easy-to-grab lentil or fish burgers. This way you can quickly prepare a delicious high-vitality lunch to take to the office, make a pretty superfood bowl to have at home, or sneak some healthy options into your kids' lunches.

# Protein-Packed Salad Nicoise
# with Balsamic Vinaigrette

I spent a year studying in Paris, and I think one of the few things I can say in French is Salade Niçoise. I adore this salad; it packs an awesome protein punch after a hard morning workout! It's so simple to make, the dressing is *délicieuse* (the other word I know in French), and it's oh-so-good for you.

---

YIELD: 2 servings          PREP TIME: 30 minutes

---

PROCEDURE

1. To make the salad dressing, combine the garlic, rosemary, olive oil, vinegar, orange juice, Dijon mustard, and honey in a high-speed blender.

2. Blend until the dressing is emulsified, about 30 seconds. Season to taste with salt and pepper.

3. Open and drain the cans of tuna. In a small bowl, combine the tuna, olive oil, garlic, red onions, cilantro, thyme, and lemon juice. Add the Scotch bonnet to taste. Season to taste with salt and pepper.

4. To assemble the salad, put the mixed greens in two beautiful bowls or plates.

5. Place the tuna mixture in the middle of the greens and the avocado, eggs, sweet potatoes, string beans, carrots, and olives around the edges.

6. Serve the dressing on the side for a perfect meal.

INGREDIENTS
FOR THE DRESSING

2 cloves garlic, minced

1 tablespoon chopped fresh rosemary, or 1 teaspoon dried

¼ cup extra-virgin olive oil

¼ cup balsamic vinegar

¼ cup fresh orange juice or water

1 tablespoon Dijon mustard

1 tablespoon honey or brown sugar

Himalayan sea salt

Ground black pepper

INGREDIENTS
FOR THE SALAD

*Listed in sidebar, opposite*

## INGREDIENTS
## FOR THE SALAD

2 (5-ounce) cans high-quality
canned tuna (in water)

2 tablespoons extra-virgin olive oil

2 cloves garlic, minced

½ medium red onion, diced

⅓ cup fresh cilantro, chopped

1 tablespoon fresh thyme, chopped,
or 1 teaspoon dried

2 tablespoons fresh lemon juice

1 Scotch bonnet or habanero
pepper, minced

Himalayan sea salt

Ground black pepper

4 cups mixed greens

¼ avocado, diced

2 hard-boiled eggs, sliced (optional)

½ cup sweet potatoes, yams, or
breadfruits, roasted and diced

¼ cup string beans, blanched

½ medium carrot, shredded

12 Nicoise olives

# Kale, Avocado, and Plantain Power Salad with Roasted Nuts and Seeds

Combine three superfoods, top them with roasted nuts and seeds, and you have a superpower salad. I love having this as a side salad or topped with grilled chicken for a satisfying meal.

| YIELD: 2 to 3 servings | PREP TIME: 20 minutes | COOK TIME: 20 minutes |
|---|---|---|

## PROCEDURE

1. Preheat the oven to 350°F.

2. Bake the plantain in a small baking dish for 20 minutes, until golden, and cut into squares.

3. Meanwhile, remove and discard the tough stems from the kale. Chop the leaves finely and put them in a large bowl.

4. Combine the olive oil, lemon juice, honey, salt, and pepper to taste in a high-speed blender for 1 minute.

5. Pour the dressing over the kale and use your hands to massage the dressing gently into the kale to soften it, 3 to 5 minutes.

6. Add the plantains and avocado to the kale and top with the roasted nuts and seeds.

## INGREDIENTS

1 small plantain, peeled

14 ounces kale

¼ cup extra-virgin olive oil

¼ cup fresh lemon juice

1 tablespoon honey or brown sugar

½ teaspoon Himalayan sea salt

Ground black pepper

¼ avocado, diced

¼ cup Roasted Nuts and Seeds (page 165)

# Green Curry Veggies with Toasted Cashew Nuts Bowl

Sometimes you just need a bowl of curry served with brown rice!
Grounding and full of warming flavors, this is comfort food at its best.

| YIELD: 2 to 4 servings | PREP TIME: 40 to 50 minutes | COOK TIME: 20 minutes |
|---|---|---|

## PROCEDURE

1. Fill a large pot with about 1 inch of water. Bring to a boil and place a steamer basket in the pot. Place the snow peas, broccoli, carrots, chocho, peppers, celery, and mushrooms in the basket, cover, and turn the heat to medium-low. Steam the vegetables until they're crisp-tender, about 3 to 5 minutes.

2. Heat a large sauté pan for 2 to 3 minutes over medium heat. Add the sesame oil and swirl to evenly coat the pan. Add the garlic, onion, and ginger to the pan and sauté for 1 minute.

3. Add the green curry paste, nutritional yeast, coconut milk, and fish sauce and cook for 2 minutes.

4. Add the steamed vegetables and sprouted mung beans and cook for another 5 minutes, until the veggies are tender.

5. Season to taste with salt and pepper, top with the cashew nuts, and enjoy!

## INGREDIENTS

1 cup snow peas, tips removed

1 cup broccoli, chopped small

2 medium carrots, diced

2 chocho (chayote) or butternut squash, diced

1 large bell pepper (yellow or red), diced

1 stalk celery, diced

1 cup shiitake, oyster, or button mushrooms, sliced

2 tablespoons sesame oil

6 cloves garlic, chopped

1 medium onion, diced

1 tablespoon grated ginger, or 1 teaspoon ground ginger

2 tablespoons green curry paste

1½ tablespoons nutritional yeast

2 cups Homemade Coconut Milk (page 159) or store-bought unsweetened coconut milk

1 teaspoon fish sauce

1 cup Sprouted Mung Beans (page 167, optional)

Himalayan sea salt

Ground black pepper

1 cup roasted cashew nuts

# Cooling Cucumber Salad
# with Roasted Chickpeas

Since Jamaica has a tropical marine climate, our average temperature year-round is about eighty degrees Fahrenheit, but in the summer it is often near ninety. The ocean breeze does help, but I like to cool it down even more with cucumbers. Not only do cucumbers keep you hydrated, but they also flush toxins, lavish you with vitamins, and fight heat from the inside out. Enjoy this fresh, crunchy salad as a meal or with your favorite protein. Prepare the roasted chickpeas while the salad is resting in the fridge.

---

**YIELD:** 2 to 4 servings **PREP TIME:** 45 minutes

---

## PROCEDURE

1. Whisk all the dressing ingredients together in a small bowl and adjust to taste.

2. Peel the cucumbers, remove the ends, and slice in half lengthwise. Scoop out the seeds with a small spoon.

3. Slice the halves into ⅛-inch-thick half-moons and transfer to a large bowl.

4. Add the peppers, onions, and cilantro to the bowl.

5. Pour the dressing over the vegetables and toss to combine.

6. Cover the bowl with a lid or plastic wrap and chill the salad for about 30 minutes in the fridge.

7. Toss the salad again before serving. Portion into bowls, top with the peanuts and chickpeas, and serve immediately.

## INGREDIENTS FOR THE DRESSING

½ cup rice wine vinegar

1 tablespoon honey

1 tablespoon sesame oil

½ teaspoon Himalayan sea salt

## INGREDIENTS FOR THE SALAD

2 medium cucumbers

1 medium red bell pepper, diced

1 medium red onion, diced

¼ cup chopped fresh cilantro

¼ cup chopped roasted peanuts

1 recipe Roasted Chickpeas Crunch (page 169)

# Raw Bok Choy Salad
# with Roasted Nuts and Seeds

This salad is easy to make and absolutely delicious! Bok choy contains almost all the essential vitamins and minerals, making it a powerhouse among vegetables. The dressing for this salad can be made ahead, so it's ready to pour anytime you get hold of some fresh, organic bok choy. It's great on callaloo, kale, and spinach too.

| YIELD: 2 to 4 servings | PREP TIME: 15 to 20 minutes | COOK TIME: 10 minutes |
| --- | --- | --- |

## PROCEDURE

1. Preheat the oven to 350°F.

2. Combine the bok choy and onions in a large bowl.

3. Spread the mixed nuts and seeds on a baking sheet and toast until golden brown, 5 to 10 minutes.

4. While the nuts are toasting, combine the vinegar and tamari in a small saucepan and bring to a boil. Remove from heat, and allow to cool, then stir in the olive oil and brown sugar.

5. Pour the dressing over the bok choy.

6. Add the roasted nuts and seeds, toss to combine, and serve.

## INGREDIENTS

2 pounds bok choy, finely chopped

1 small red onion, diced

¼ cup mixed nuts and seeds (such as sliced almonds, pumpkin seeds, sunflower seeds, sesame seeds)

½ cup apple cider vinegar

¼ cup wheat-free tamari

¼ cup extra-virgin olive oil

¼ cup brown sugar or honey

# Suzie's Famous Tabbouleh Salad

I'm married to a Lebanese man and the first thing I had to do after we got married was learn how to make hummus and tabbouleh! My sister-in-law Suzie is more than a sister; she is the head honcho of the Feanny family kitchen in Miami. When we visit Grandma Norma, my wonderful mother-in-law, there is always a huge bowl of tabbouleh waiting for us, made lovingly by Suzie. Here is her precious recipe. Parsley is so good for you. Not only does it improve digestion, fight cancer, and act as a natural diuretic, but it also has antibacterial and antifungal properties. If you like, substitute the bulgur wheat with grated cauliflower or quinoa, and carrots for the tomatoes. Be sure to use the best quality olive oil you can find.

---

YIELD: 4 to 5 servings          PREP TIME: 40 to 45 minutes

---

## PROCEDURE

1. Take a comfortable seat in the kitchen and mindfully pick the parsley and mint by taking the leaves off the stems, then wash thoroughly and dry in a salad spinner. Chop the leaves finely. Set aside.

2. Rinse, then soak the bulgur in hot water for 10 minutes, then drain thoroughly.

3. Put the tomatoes over the drained bulgur for about 5 minutes so it absorbs the tomato juice.

4. In a large bowl, mix the bulgur and herbs together with the onions, scallions, lemon juice, olive oil, salt, cinnamon, allspice, and pepper.

5. To serve, arrange the lettuce leaves in a shallow bowl or on a platter and spoon the tabbouleh on top.

6. Try to leave some for everyone else!

## INGREDIENTS

1 pound curly parsley

1 pound flat-leaf parsley

¼ pound mint

½ cup extra-fine bulgur wheat, or ½ cup cooked quinoa, or 1 cup grated cauliflower

4 firm medium tomatoes, diced

1 red onion, diced

2 stalks of finely chopped scallions

½ cup fresh lemon juice

½ cup extra-virgin olive oil

1 teaspoon Himalayan sea salt

1 pinch cinnamon

1 pinch allspice

1 pinch ground black pepper

Lettuce leaves, for serving

## TRY A SUPERFOOD BOWL

Combine tabbouleh and Spicy Mediterranean Lentil Salad (page 81) with some Herbed Avocado Hummus (page 119), Savory Flaxseed Crackers (page 131), and Pickled Beets with Pimento and Scotch Bonnet (page 173) for a perfect Mediterranean superfood bowl.

# Pretty Purple and White Cabbage Salad with Cranberries

An Indian sage once told me to eat all the colors of the rainbow each day. This salad has four of them—purple, white, orange, and red. The colors together are so beautiful.

---

YIELD: 2 to 4 servings          PREP TIME: 20 to 30 minutes

---

## PROCEDURE

1. In a small bowl, whisk all the dressing ingredients together. Season to taste with salt and pepper.

2. Trim off the stem of each cabbage.

3. Quarter the cabbages and cut out the thick white cores.

4. Thinly slice the cabbage using a sharp knife or the slicing disk in a food processor or a mandoline. You should end up with about 2 cup purple cabbage and 4 cups white.

5. Toss the cabbage and carrots together in a large bowl.

6. Add the cranberries.

7. When ready to serve, pour the dressing over the salad, and toss. Tastes even better the next day!

## INGREDIENTS FOR THE DRESSING

½ cup fresh lemon juice

¼ cup extra-virgin olive oil

1 tablespoon brown sugar or honey

Himalayan sea salt

Ground black pepper

## INGREDIENTS FOR THE SALAD

½ small head purple cabbage (about 2 cups)

1 small head white or green cabbage (about 4 cups)

2 medium carrots, shredded (about 1 cup)

2 tablespoons dried cranberries, chopped

# Daikon and Carrot Salad

I recently discovered daikon, a large white radish readily available in Jamaica and in Asian markets in the US, and I'm in love. Not only is it anti-inflammatory and immune boosting, but it's also a perfect detox food as it is known to clean the kidneys.

YIELD: 2 to 4 servings          PREP TIME: 30 minutes

## PROCEDURE

1. Shave the daikon into ribbons with a vegetable peeler or spiralizer.

2. Toss with ¼ teaspoon salt in a colander, then let drain in the sink for 5 minutes.

3. Meanwhile, shave or spiralize the carrots into ribbons.

4. Combine the ginger, vinegar, lemon juice, and the remaining salt in a large bowl.

5. Slowly whisk in the vegetable oil and sesame oil until blended.

6. Toss the daikon and carrots with the dressing. Add more salt to taste.

7. Sprinkle the sesame seeds on top and serve.

## INGREDIENTS

1½ pounds daikon, peeled

¾ teaspoon Himalayan sea salt, divided

1 pound carrots, peeled

1 tablespoon grated fresh ginger

3 tablespoons rice wine vinegar

2 teaspoons fresh lemon or lime juice

¼ cup vegetable oil

1 teaspoon sesame oil

¾ teaspoon white sesame seeds, toasted

¾ teaspoon black sesame seeds

# Black-Eyed Peas, Parsley, and Cherry Tomato Salad

This winning combo of plant-based protein and detoxifying parsley will keep you coming back for more. Sometimes I eat it for breakfast—it's that good!

| YIELD: 10 servings | PREP TIME: 30 minutes active prep + overnight soaking of the peas | COOK TIME: 30 minutes |
|---|---|---|

## PROCEDURE

1. Put the peas in a large pot and cover with about 4 inches of water. Soak the peas overnight, drain the water, and rinse.

2. To cook the peas, cover them with fresh water plus about another 2 inches, bring to a boil, and let simmer for 15 to 20 minutes, or until peas are tender. Drain, then let cool.

3. In a medium bowl, combine the lemon juice, garlic, sugar, mustard, salt, and pepper. Whisk in the olive oil until ingredients are thoroughly combined.

4. Add the black-eyed peas and onions, and toss to coat with the dressing.

5. Cover with plastic wrap and leave in the fridge for an hour to marinate.

6. When you are ready to serve, add the tomatoes and chopped parsley to the marinated black-eyed pea mixture.

7. Add a little more salt and pepper to taste.

8. Garnish with the sprigs of parsley and serve.

## INGREDIENTS

⅔ cup dried black-eyed peas

¼ cup fresh lemon juice

2 cloves garlic, minced

2 teaspoons brown sugar or honey

1 teaspoon Dijon mustard

½ teaspoon Himalayan sea salt, plus more as needed

½ teaspoon ground black pepper, plus more as needed

¼ cup extra-virgin olive oil

1 medium red onion, diced

1 cup halved cherry tomatoes

¼ pound curly parsley, finely chopped, plus a few sprigs for garnish

# Roasted Beet, Orange, Feta, and Rosemary Salad

I don't include a lot of dairy in my cooking, but the feta completes
this recipe because it balances the flavors and textures perfectly. The salad,
which has become a family favorite, is festive and so pretty. Be sure to add
the oranges at the last minute so they don't absorb the color of the beets.

| YIELD: 4 to 6 servings | PREP TIME: 40 minutes | COOK TIME: 40 minutes |
| --- | --- | --- |

## PROCEDURE

1. Preheat the oven to 350°F.

2. Peel the beets, chop into squares (you should end up with about 8 cups), transfer to a large bowl, and season to taste with salt and pepper.

3. Stir in 2 tablespoons of the olive oil, ½ of the chopped rosemary, and half of the minced garlic. Transfer the mixture to a large rimmed baking sheet.

4. Roast for 40 minutes, until the beets are firm but easily pierced by a fork. Let cool.

5. Peel and cut the oranges into segments, removing all the white parts. Set aside.

6. Mix the vinegar and honey with the remaining olive oil, rosemary, and garlic in a high-speed blender or food processor. Blend for 20 seconds, until well combined.

7. Pour the dressing over the cooled beets, add the orange segments, and top with the feta cheese.

## INGREDIENTS

4 pounds beets

Himalayan sea salt

Ground black pepper

¼ cup extra-virgin olive oil, divided

Leaves from 2 long stalks rosemary, chopped, divided

3 cloves garlic, minced, divided

2 medium oranges

¼ cup aged balsamic vinegar

1 tablespoon honey

½ cup feta cheese, crumbled

# Superfood Cilantro-Lime Grilled Salmon

I'm dating myself by sharing this story, but what the hell! In 1986, the summer
I graduated from college, I hitchhiked from Florida to Alaska to work in a salmon factory.
That is a whole different book that one day I'll write, but it's probably the reason I love
salmon so much. Not only is it one of the most nutritious foods on the planet, but it's also
packed with omega-3 fatty acids that help to reduce inflammation, lower blood pressure,
and decrease the risk of heart disease. If you eat salmon frequently, it's better to buy
wild-caught instead of farm-raised salmon to minimize exposure to harmful toxins.

| YIELD: 4 servings | PREP TIME: 70 minutes | COOK TIME: 10 minutes |
| --- | --- | --- |

## PROCEDURE

1. Wash the salmon, pat dry with a paper towel, and put the fillets in a shallow dish.

2. Put all the other ingredients in a small bowl, mix thoroughly, and pour over the salmon, making sure to cover the fillets.

3. Cover with foil and place in the fridge to marinate for about 30 minutes.

4. Preheat a grill on high heat.

5. Grill the salmon for 3 to 5 minutes on each side, until fillets are opaque in the center and flake easily.

## INGREDIENTS

4 (3- to 4-ounce) salmon fillets, or a small side of salmon cut into 4-ounce pieces

½ cup chopped fresh cilantro

4 cloves garlic, minced

¼ cup fresh lime juice

¼ cup extra-virgin olive oil

1 teaspoon Dijon mustard

1 teaspoon Himalayan sea salt

½ teaspoon ground black pepper

# Spicy Mediterranean Lentil Salad

Although this is a salad, I often serve it as a main dish with Suzie's Famous Tabbouleh Salad (page 72), Herbed Avocado Hummus (page 119), and Savory Flaxseed Crackers (page 131) alongside for a delicious high-vitality Mediterranean vegetarian meal.

| YIELD: 6 to 8 servings | PREP TIME: 45 minutes active prep + 2 hours soaking | COOK TIME: 15 minutes |
|---|---|---|

## PROCEDURE

1. Soak lentils for 2 hours.

2. Rinse and drain the lentils.

3. Bring 3 cups of liquid and the lentils to a boil in a large saucepan (note that lentils will double or triple in size as they cook). Cover the pan tightly, reduce the heat, and simmer until the lentils are tender, 10 to 15 minutes. Remove from the heat and rinse with cold water to cool.

4. In a large bowl, combine the kale, bell peppers, onions, scallions, carrots, hot peppers, and celery.

5. For the dressing, pour the lemon juice, garlic, olive oil, honey, salt, and pepper to taste into a bottle and shake well to combine.

6. Add the cooked lentils to the vegetables, pour the dressing on top, and stir till fully mixed. Garnish with the cilantro and serve.

## INGREDIENTS

1 cup dried lentils

3 cups water

1 cup kale, chopped

1 cup chopped bell pepper

½ cup chopped red onion

2 whole scallions, sliced

½ cup chopped carrots

¼ Scotch bonnet or habanero pepper, seeded and minced

½ cup chopped celery

½ cup fresh lemon juice

2 cloves garlic, minced

¼ cup extra-virgin olive oil

1 ½ tablespoons honey

1 teaspoon Himalayan sea salt

Ground black pepper

½ cup finely chopped fresh cilantro

Superfood Cilantro-Lime Grilled Salmon, page 80, and Carrot-Ginger Zinger Dressing, page 179

# Callaloo, Pumpkin, and Lentil Burgers

I wanted to create a vegetarian burger that could freeze well and that I could pop in the oven for a quick and healthy lunch. We make these burgers in batches and freeze them in packages of two. I love to top them with Jerked Almond Pâté (page 126), and serve them with my Pretty Purple and White Cabbage Salad with Cranberries (page 74) and Baked Coconut-Infused Bammy Chips or Croutons (page 168) on the side. Yum!

| YIELD: 24 (2-ounce) burgers | PREP TIME: 30 minutes + overnight soaking | COOK TIME: 30 minutes |
|---|---|---|

PROCEDURE

1. Soak the lentils overnight.

2. Rinse and drain the lentils.

3. Preheat the oven to 350°F.

4. Fill two saucepans with 1 cup of water each. Add the lentils to one pan and the millet to the other. Bring to a boil, lower the heat, and simmer lentils and millet for 20 minutes, until lentils and millet are tender.

5. While the lentils and millet are cooking, heat a large sauté pan over medium heat for 2 to 3 minutes. Add the coconut oil and swirl to evenly coat the pan. Sauté the onions and garlic until brown.

6. Add the pumpkin, carrots, celery, hot peppers, salt, black pepper to taste, and callaloo.

7. Cook for 5 minutes, stirring occasionally.

8. Add the cooked lentils and millet, nutritional yeast, and almond flour and cook for 5 more minutes.

9. Remove from the heat and let cool.

INGREDIENTS

14 ounces dried lentils

¼ cup whole-grain millet

3 cups water, divided

2 tablespoons coconut oil

⅛ cup chopped onions

1 clove garlic, minced

1 cup shredded pumpkin or butternut squash

¼ cup shredded carrots

½ stalk celery, chopped

¼ Scotch bonnet or habanero pepper, seeded and chopped

¼ cup callaloo or spinach

1 teaspoon nutritional yeast

⅛ cup almond flour

1 teaspoon Himalayan sea salt

Ground black pepper

10. Once the mixture is cool, form it into 24 (3-ounce) burgers. Place them on a baking sheet.

11. Bake the burgers for 25 to 30 minutes, until golden brown.

12. Remove from the oven and let cool, unless you plan to eat them right away.

13. These burgers can be stored in the freezer. To prepare frozen burgers, simply take as many as you'll be eating out of the freezer, rub with olive or coconut oil, and bake at 350°F for 15–20 minutes, until heated through.

## SCOTCH BONNET PEPPERS

Scotch bonnet peppers are small, very hot peppers that are native to the Caribbean and widely available there. A good substitute if Scotch bonnets aren't available in your grocery store is the habanero pepper. Both Scotch bonnet and habanero peppers pack a lot of punch, so feel free to adjust the quantity called for in a recipe to your liking.

# Simple Grilled Sesame Snapper with Pineapple, Cilantro, and Scotch Bonnet Salsa

The fishermen in Montego Bay know to call me when they have freshly caught snapper. Nothing is more delicious than simple grilled fish with a spicy topping, served with a great salad and grilled plantains. You can use any fish you like here!

| YIELD: 4 servings | PREP TIME: 20 to 30 minutes | COOK TIME: 20 minutes |
| --- | --- | --- |

## PROCEDURE

1. Rinse the fish and pat dry with a paper towel.

2. Mix the sesame oil, ginger, garlic, brown sugar, and tamari together in a small bowl. Add salt and pepper to taste.

3. Rub the snapper with mixture and marinate in the fridge for 1 to 2 hours.

4. Preheat a grill to medium.

5. Grill the fish for 15 to 20 minutes, until it becomes opaque and flakes easily.

6. Serve the grilled fish with Pineapple, Cilantro, and Scotch Bonnet Salsa.

## INGREDIENTS

2 pounds snapper (1 whole fish or 4 fillets)

2 tablespoons sesame oil

1 tablespoon minced ginger

1 tablespoon minced garlic

1 teaspoon brown sugar

2 tablespoons wheat-free tamari

Himalayan sea salt

Ground black pepper

1 recipe Pineapple, Cilantro, and Scotch Bonnet Salsa (page 172)

## A TIP FOR COOKING FISH

Here's how to tell if fish is done: poke the tines of a fork into the thickest portion of the fish at a 45-degree angle. Gently twist the fork and pull up some of the fish. Undercooked fish resists flaking and is translucent. Fish that's done is opaque and flakes easily.

# Jerk Chicken or Black Bean, Plantain, and Avocado Rice Wraps

Sometimes you have to wrap it all up! I discovered these rice wraps in Bali and have never looked back. Don't panic—if I can learn to make them, so can you. It may take a couple tries to get the wrapping technique down, but once you have that, they're easy. Experiment with your own combinations, but this one is the best. If you want a veggie version, try it with some Jerk-Infused Black Beans (page 91).

| YIELD: 2 servings | PREP TIME: 30 to 35 minutes | COOK TIME: 25 minutes |
| --- | --- | --- |

## PROCEDURE

1. Preheat the oven to 400°F.

2. Cut plantain on the diagonal to make ½-inch-thick slices.

3. Place the plantain slices in a bowl, add the oil, and toss gently to coat them.

4. Arrange the plantain slices on a baking sheet and bake 15 minutes, then flip and bake another 10 minutes, until golden brown.

5. Remove from the oven, let cool, and cut into fine strips.

6. Mix cabbage, carrots, string beans, and cilantro in a large bowl. Add the Jerked Almond Pâté and stir until all the vegetables are moistened.

7. Dab the rice wraps on both sides with a little water and spread them flat on a large cutting board.

8. Put one kale or bok choy leaf on top of each rice wrap, then divide the vegetable mixture evenly between them. Finish with even portions of grilled chicken or black beans, plantains, and avocado.

## INGREDIENTS

½ medium plantain

1 tablespoon coconut oil

½ pound Chinese or green cabbage, shredded

1 medium carrot, shredded

¼ pound string beans, cut into fine strips

½ cup chopped fresh cilantro

¼ cup Jerked Almond Pâté (page 126)

4 rice paper wrappers

4 large kale or bok choy leaves

4 medium-sized grilled chicken breasts, sliced, or 1 recipe Jerk-Infused Black Beans (page 91)

½ medium avocado, thinly sliced lengthwise

9. Roll up each wrap and secure with foil or plastic wrap.

10. Cut each wrap into 2 pieces and serve with Asian Dipping Sauce for Everything (page 184) and a great salad (the Daikon and Carrot Salad, page 76, is my favorite).

## WRAPPING HOW-TO

1. Dip rice paper in warm water for about 3 to 4 seconds, until rice paper becomes moistened with water. After dipping your rice paper in warm water, lay wrapper onto your work surface. Allow rice paper to soak up water and become soft and pliable ( about 30 seconds to 1 minute) before you start to roll.

2. Starting in the center of the wrapper, place the first few pieces of filling in a rectangular shape, staying away from the edges of the wrapper.

3. Continue to add all of the fillings, maintaining the rectangle shape in the middle.

4. Work quickly; you don't want your wrapper to fall apart. When you've placed all of your ingredients in a nice little pile in the middle of the wrapper, it's time to roll it shut!

5. Be careful not to overfill your wrapper because it will cause the rice paper to tear.

6. Start by folding the top and bottom sections of the rice paper in over the vegetables.

7. Starting on the left-hand side, stretch the left side of the wrapper around the pile of ingredients, tucking and rolling until you can rest the wrapper just under the ingredients.

8. Tuck the corners in and then continue to roll, making your roll as tight as possible without ripping the rice paper wrapper.

9. That's it, you just rolled your very own wrap!

Jerk Chicken or Black Bean, Plantain, and Avocado Rice Wraps, page 88, and Raw Bok Choy Salad with Roasted Nuts and Seeds, page 71

# Jerk-Infused Black Beans

These jerk-infused black beans are a spicy vegan alternative to chicken.
The fiber, potassium, folate, vitamin B6, and phytonutrient content
of black beans, along with their lack of cholesterol, all support heart health.
These are delicious with brown rice too.

| YIELD: 4 servings | PREP TIME: 1 hour 30 minutes + overnight soaking of the black beans | COOK TIME: 90 minutes |
|---|---|---|

## PROCEDURE

1. Soak the black beans in a large pot of water overnight.

2. The next day, rinse the beans, cover with the water, and bring to a boil over high heat. Reduce the heat and simmer, covered, for 30 minutes, skimming off any foam.

3. Stir in the onions and simmer 30 minutes more.

4. Add the jerk seasoning, garlic, oregano, cumin, and red pepper flakes. Simmer, uncovered, for 30 minutes, stirring occasionally, until tender.

5. Stir in the brown sugar and vinegar. Taste before seasoning with salt and pepper.

6. Turn the beans out into a large serving bowl and garnish with the scallions.

## INGREDIENTS

½ pound dried black beans

3 cups water

1 medium onion, chopped

2 teaspoons jerk seasoning

3 cloves garlic, minced

½ teaspoon dried oregano

½ teaspoon ground cumin

Pinch red pepper flakes

2 teaspoons brown sugar

2 tablespoons white wine vinegar

Himalayan sea salt

Ground black pepper

2 whole scallions, chopped, for garnish

# Toby's Cuban Lime-Soaked Chicken

I love all things Cuban. In fact, my daughter's name is Toby Cuba! This recipe was given to me when I visited that beautiful island years ago, and we've been making it ever since. Toby requests it every time she comes home from college. She loves it best with Sweet Coconut Brown Rice and Gungo Peas (page 97), Pretty Purple and White Cabbage Salad with Cranberries (page 74), and a side of Holy Holy Guacamole (page 123).

| YIELD: 2 to 4 servings | PREP TIME: 20 to 25 minutes | COOK TIME: 30 minutes |
|---|---|---|

## PROCEDURE

1. Wash the chicken with the two tablespoons of lime juice, remove the chicken skin, and let it drain. Place the chicken in a shallow dish.

2. In a small bowl, combine the garlic, thyme, lime juice, brown sugar, salt, and pepper and pour over the chicken. Marinate for 3 to 4 hours in the refrigerator, covered in plastic wrap.

3. Preheat a grill to medium.

4. Grill the chicken for about 25 to 30 minutes, turning once, until fully cooked (internal temperature of the chicken should be at least 165°F; chicken should not have any pink, and juices should run clear).

5. Use the leftovers (if you have any) to make a fabulous salad! Add the chicken to a bed of mixed greens with black beans, avocado, corn and tomatoes and top with the Pineapple, Rosemary, and Ginger Dressing (page 177)—delicious!

## INGREDIENTS

2 pounds chicken parts, bone-in

¾ cup plus 2 tablespoons fresh lime or lemon juice, divided

1 whole head garlic, minced

¼ cup fresh thyme, chopped, or 4 teaspoons dried

1 tablespoon brown sugar or honey

1 teaspoon Himalayan sea salt

1 teaspoon ground black pepper

Sweet Coconut Brown Rice and Gungo Peas, page 97, and Toby's Cuban Lime-Soaked Chicken, page 93

# Sweet Coconut Brown Rice and Gungo Peas

Everyone loves rice and peas in Jamaica, but I elevated this version to include brown instead of white rice and gungo peas (pigeon peas) instead of kidney beans, which are less starchy and have more protein. Cooking it in a little homemade coconut milk makes it even more delicious.

| YIELD: 5 to 6 servings | PREP TIME: 15 minutes active prep + overnight soaking of the peas | COOK TIME: 50 minutes |
| --- | --- | --- |

## PROCEDURE

1. Soak the peas overnight in a large pot of water.

2. The next day, rinse the peas, cover with the water, and bring to a boil. Turn the heat down to low and simmer for 30 minutes, until the peas are tender.

3. Rinse the brown rice and add it to the peas. Stir in the coconut milk, thyme, garlic, hot pepper, and salt.

4. Simmer for another 20 minutes, until the rice is tender yet firm. Add a little extra water if needed.

5. Garnish with scallions and serve.

## INGREDIENTS

1 cup dried gungo peas (pigeon peas)

3 cups water, plus more as needed

2 cups short-grain brown rice

2 cups Homemade Coconut Milk (page 159) or store-bought unsweetened coconut milk

1 tablespoon fresh thyme, chopped

5 cloves garlic, minced

1 whole Scotch bonnet pepper, chopped

½ teaspoon Himalayan sea salt

3 whole scallions, chopped, for garnish

# Spicy Mahi-Mahi Fish Burgers

If you get hold of some fresh mahi-mahi (or any fish with a firm texture, such as kingfish or wahoo), make these fish burgers that your entire family will love. They freeze beautifully too. Pair with Healthy Sweet Potato "Cheesy" Fries (page 115) and a fresh salad for a great summer meal.

| YIELD: 24 (2-ounce) burgers | PREP TIME: 1 hour | COOK TIME: 30 minutes |
| --- | --- | --- |

## PROCEDURE

1. Preheat the oven to 350°F.

2. In a large pot, bring the water, thyme, and ginger to a boil and add the fish. Boil for about 12 minutes. When fish reaches the proper cooking temperature, it will be opaque and flake easily.

3. Remove the fish, let cool, and very carefully remove the skin and the meat from the bones. Be sure to double-check for tiny bones!

4. In a large bowl, crumble the fish meat. Add the coconut oil, cranberries, bell peppers, onions, corn, carrots, celery, cilantro, hot peppers, nutritional yeast, garlic powder, salt, and pepper. Mix well.

5. Add the eggs and almond meal and mix until thoroughly combined.

6. Form into 24 (3-ounce) burgers.

7. Bake in the oven for 25 to 30 minutes, until golden brown.

8. Serve with Simple Lemon-Tahini Dipping Sauce (page 181), Herbed Avocado Hummus (page 119), or Jerked Almond Pâté (page 126) on top.

## INGREDIENTS

3 cups water

1 sprig fresh thyme

1 (3-inch) knob ginger, peeled

2 pounds mahi-mahi

1 tablespoon coconut oil, melted

¼ cup dried cranberries, chopped

½ cup finely chopped bell pepper, any color

1 medium red onion, chopped

1 ear corn, cooked and kernels removed from cob

1 cup shredded carrots

2 stalks celery and leaves, diced

½ cup finely chopped fresh cilantro

¼ Scotch Bonnet pepper or habanero pepper, seeded and minced

1 tablespoon nutritional yeast

1 teaspoon garlic powder

1 teaspoon Himalayan sea salt

1 teaspoon ground black pepper

2 large eggs

½ cup almond meal

9. Freeze extra burgers in a shallow covered container. To reheat, place frozen burgers on aluminum foil and bake for 20 to 30 minutes at 350°F until heated through.

**NOTE:** Check out *A Tip for Cooking Fish* on page 87.

### WHY RINSE QUINOA?

Rinsing removes quinoa's natural coating, called saponin, which can make it taste bitter or soapy. Although boxed quinoa is often prerinsed, it doesn't hurt to give the seeds an additional rinse at home.

# Savory Rainbow Quinoa with Roasted Beets, Callaloo, Pumpkin, and Cherry Tomatoes

Quinoa is an ancient grain and modern superfood hero. I love its nutty flavor and protein punch. Filled with all the colors of the rainbow, this dish is both beautiful and versatile: serve it hot or cold as a main or a side.

| YIELD: 2 to 4 servings | PREP TIME: 25 minutes | COOK TIME: 35 minutes |
| --- | --- | --- |

## PROCEDURE

1. Preheat the oven to 350°F. Line a large baking sheet with aluminum foil.

2. Rinse the quinoa and leave to drain.

3. Combine beets, pumpkin, cherry tomatoes, olive oil, rosemary, thyme, and sea salt in a large bowl and toss together gently.

4. Transfer the mixture to the prepared baking sheet and roast in the oven for about 35 minutes, until vegetables are tender.

5. While the vegetables are roasting, combine the quinoa and the water in a medium saucepan. Bring to a boil. Cover, reduce heat to low, and simmer until the quinoa is tender and water is absorbed, about 15 minutes.

6. Combine the cooked quinoa with the roasted vegetables, callaloo, Scotch bonnet pepper to taste, and cilantro. Stir gently.

## INGREDIENTS

1 cup quinoa

1 cup diced beets

1 cup diced pumpkin or butternut squash

1 cup halved cherry tomatoes

1 tablespoon extra-virgin olive oil

2 tablespoons chopped fresh rosemary, or 2 teaspoons dried

1 tablespoon fresh thyme, chopped, or 1 teaspoon dried

1 pinch Himalayan sea salt

1 cup water

¼ cup shredded callaloo (or spinach or kale)

Scotch bonnet or habanero pepper, minced, to taste

¼ cup fresh cilantro, chopped

# Italian Raw Pasta with Zucchini, Chocho, and Carrots

You have to purchase a spiralizer for your kitchen—it just makes everything look so pretty. It's also great for making this fabulous vegan raw pasta dish. Nutritional yeast adds a yummy creamy flavor—you won't miss the Parmesan cheese one bit. Chocho (also known as chayote) is a gourd that can typically be found at Hispanic grocery stores or sourced online. You can also use squash, beets, and pumpkin if you prefer. I like to roast the tomatoes while I spiralize the veggies; then, once the sauce is ready, pour it over the veggies and sautéed mushrooms.

| YIELD: 2 to 4 servings | PREP TIME: 30 minutes | COOK TIME: 40 minutes |
|---|---|---|

## PROCEDURE

1. Put zucchini, carrots, and chocho through a spiralizer to make pasta. (If you don't own a spiralizer, use a vegetable peeler to make long ribbons.) You should end up with about 1½ cups zucchini and 1 cup each carrots and chocho.

2. Place spiralized veggies in a large bowl.

3. Heat a large sauté pan over medium heat for 2 to 3 minutes. Add the olive oil and swirl to evenly coat the pan. Add the mushrooms and peppers and gently sauté them until lightly browned, about 4 to 5 minutes.

4. If it's not already hot (i.e., if you're not making the tomato sauce simultaneously), warm the tomato sauce in a large saucepan over medium heat.

5. Mix the sautéed mushrooms into the warm tomato sauce and pour this mixture over the spiralized veggies. This will cook the veggies slightly. Top with the olives, then sprinkle with the nutritional yeast for a nice cheesy taste!

6. Garnish with the basil leaves and serve while hot.

## INGREDIENTS

1 large or 2 medium zucchini

1 large or 2 medium carrots

2 medium chocho (chayote)

2 tablespoons extra-virgin olive oil

1 cup sliced fresh shiitake, oyster, or button mushrooms

Scotch bonnet or habanero pepper, minced

1 recipe Kid-Friendly Superfood Roasted Tomato Sauce (page 162)

Handful black olives, sliced, for garnish

2 tablespoons nutritional yeast

Handful basil leaves, for garnish

# Mary Jane's Grilled Eggplant Salad
# with Yogurt, Mint, and Pomegranate Molasses

My sister-in-law Mary Jane is a miracle worker in the kitchen. Like, literally, she can whip up a gourmet meal for twenty-five people in a few hours and make it look like she's not even trying. And she does it all with the most beautiful smile you could ever imagine. Her food is so full of love! Enjoy this eggplant recipe Mary Jane shared with me. It's a winner.

| YIELD: 4 to 6 servings | PREP TIME: 20 minutes | COOK TIME: 40 minutes |
| --- | --- | --- |

## PROCEDURE

1. Preheat the oven to 375°F.

2. In a medium bowl toss the eggplant with 2 tablespoons of the olive oil and season to taste with salt.

3. Transfer to a large baking sheet and roast in the oven for 40 minutes, or until the eggplant is tender.

4. Heat a large sauté pan over medium heat for 2 to 3 minutes. Add the remaining olive oil and swirl to evenly coat the pan. Sauté the garlic for 30 seconds, then remove the garlic from the pan and add the yogurt, mint, molasses, and salt to taste.

5. Just before serving, place the eggplant on a platter and spoon the yogurt mixture on top until each piece is covered.

6. Garnish with the pine nuts and fresh pomegranate seeds.

7. Serve either chilled or at room temperature.

## INGREDIENTS

2 large Italian eggplant, peeled and cubed

4 tablespoons extra-virgin olive oil, divided

Himalayan sea salt

2 cloves garlic, crushed

2 cups plain Greek yogurt

1 tablespoon dried black mint, crushed (don't substitute peppermint)

2 tablespoons pomegranate molasses

1 tablespoon pine nuts, toasted, for garnish

Fresh pomegranate seeds, for garnish

# Curried Mung Bean
# Wrapped in Bok Choy Leaves

Used extensively in Indian cooking, mung beans are easily digestible and packed with protein as well as nutrients such as potassium, magnesium, folate, copper, zinc, and B vitamins. I just love them, and wrapping them in bok choy leaves and serving them with Asian dipping sauce will blow you away. Make extra beans to have on hand when you need to prep a quick meal: they're delicious on just about everything!

| YIELD: 8 to 10 wraps | PREP TIME: 20 minutes active prep + overnight soaking of the beans | COOK TIME: 35 minutes |
| --- | --- | --- |

## PROCEDURE

1. Soak the mung beans overnight in a medium pot of water.

2. The next day, heat a large sauté pan over medium heat for 2 to 3 minutes. Add the olive oil and swirl to evenly coat the pan. Sauté the onions, garlic, thyme, scallions, and curry powder.

3. Drain the mung beans, then add them and the coconut milk to the onion mixture.

4. Cook for about 25 minutes, until the beans are tender, adding water as needed.

5. Add the carrots, string beans, and nutritional yeast and cook for 10 minutes. Stir in the cilantro, remove from the heat, and let stand.

6. Dip each bok choy leaf in a bowl of hot water for 20 seconds, rinse with cold water, and dry with a paper towel. Spread the leaves on a clean surface.

## INGREDIENTS

1 cup dried mung beans

2 tablespoons extra-virgin olive oil

½ cup chopped onions

3 cloves garlic, minced

1 tablespoon fresh thyme, chopped, or 1 teaspoon dried

2 whole scallions, chopped

1 teaspoon Indian curry powder

1 cup Homemade Coconut Milk (page 159) or ½ (16-ounce) can store-bought unsweetened coconut milk

½ cup diced carrots

½ cup chopped string beans

1 tablespoon nutritional yeast

¼ cup fresh cilantro, chopped

8 to 10 large bok choy leaves

1 recipe Asian Dipping Sauce for Everything (page 184) or Simple Lemon-Tahini Dipping Sauce (page 181), for serving

7. Scoop 1 full tablespoon of the cooked beans onto the center of each leaf and roll it up, folding in the outer edges as you go along.

8. Serve with Asian Dipping Sauce for Everything (page 184).

# Steamed Yard Food with a Twist

We are so blessed in Jamaica with our yard food: the breadfruits, green bananas, and endless varieties of yams growing in abundance all around us! We are in complex-carbohydrate heaven. I used to believe that carbs were bad for you, but now I know that, in moderation (three servings per day), they give you the energy you need to live fit, live life, and live love. Just ask Usain Bolt. Here's a recipe that my friends and family love. You can use breadfruits, yams, or both.

| YIELD: 8 to 10 servings | PREP TIME: 10 minutes | COOK TIME: 15 minutes |
|---|---|---|

## PROCEDURE

1. Fill a large pot with about 1 inch of water. Bring to a boil and place a steamer basket in the pot. Place the breadfruit in the basket, cover, and turn the heat to medium-low. Steam the breadfruit until fully cooked (it will be tender but still firm), about 12 to 15 minutes or until the flesh is easily pierced with a fork. Let cool.

2. When the breadfruit has cooled, combine it with the coconut milk, coconut oil, nutritional yeast, paprika, and sea salt in a large bowl. Stir gently. The finished texture will be somewhat chunky.

3. Serve with Scotch Bonnet Cashew Cream Cheese (page 124) or Herbed Avocado Hummus (page 119).

## INGREDIENTS

1 large breadfruit, cubed (6 to 7 cups)

1 cup Homemade Coconut Milk (page 159) or ½ (16-ounce) can store-bought unsweetened coconut milk

2 tablespoons coconut oil

2 tablespoons nutritional yeast

1 teaspoon smoked paprika

1 pinch Himalayan sea salt

Franny's Blessed Hummus, page 121

# Roasted Curried Cauliflower

Looking for a delicious side dish to spice things up a bit? This is it!
Roast a bunch of veggies at the beginning of the week so you can toss them
into another dish anytime you like—a great way to get in your veggies.

| YIELD: 2 to 3 servings | PREP TIME: 15 minutes | COOK TIME: 20 minutes |
| --- | --- | --- |

## PROCEDURE

1. In a large bowl, cover the cauliflower with salted water and soak for 10 minutes.

2. Drain the cauliflower, pat dry, and return it to the bowl.

3. In a small bowl, mix together all the remaining ingredients. Rub the mixture onto the cauliflower.

4. Marinate for 15 minutes.

5. Meanwhile, preheat the oven to 400°F or a grill to medium heat.

6. Transfer the cauliflower to a large baking sheet, being careful not to overcrowd the pan. (If you're grilling the cauliflower, skip this step and place the cauliflower directly on the grill.) Roast in the oven for 15 to 20 minutes or on the grill for 5 to 10 minutes, until golden brown and crunchy.

## INGREDIENTS

2 pounds cauliflower, cut into big chunks (about 3 cups)

½ teaspoon Himalayan sea salt for the salted water plus ½ teaspoon for the seasoning

½ teaspoon curry powder

½ teaspoon ground cumin

½ teaspoon ground coriander

½ teaspoon garlic powder

1 teaspoon nutritional yeast

½ teaspoon ground black pepper

3 tablespoons extra-virgin olive oil

# Grilled Cabbage

Sometimes the simplest things in life are the best. You may not have thought of grilling cabbage, so I've included this recipe. We grill all kinds of veggies, but my family loves this dish the most; it tastes amazing with everything.

| YIELD: 4 to 5 servings | PREP TIME: 60 minutes | COOK TIME: 15 minutes |
| --- | --- | --- |

## PROCEDURE

1. In a small bowl, combine the olive oil, garlic powder, cumin, coriander, nutritional yeast, salt, and pepper. Put the cabbage in a large bowl and rub the mixture into the cabbage.

2. Cover with plastic wrap and marinate in the fridge for 40 to 45 minutes.

3. Preheat the grill to medium.

4. Grill the cabbage directly on the grill for 10 to 15 minutes, until it's mostly tender but still crunchy in the center.

## INGREDIENTS

1 teaspoon extra-virgin olive oil

1 teaspoon garlic powder

1 teaspoon ground cumin

1 teaspoon ground coriander

1 teaspoon nutritional yeast

½ teaspoon Himalayan sea salt

½ teaspoon ground black pepper

2 medium heads cabbage, quartered

# Raw Broccoli Tahini Salad

A little creamy, a little sweet, and very crunchy, this side dish is good for the heart, mind, and body! It's packed with B vitamins, omega-3 fatty acids, protein, zinc, calcium, and iron.

YIELD: 2 to 3 servings     PREP TIME: 20 to 30 minutes

## PROCEDURE

1. Combine the broccoli, garlic, sesame seeds, onions, and cranberries in a large bowl.

2. Add the Simple Lemon-Tahini Dipping Sauce. Stir gently to combine.

## INGREDIENTS

3 small heads broccoli, cut into bite-size florets

3 cloves garlic, minced

2 tablespoons black or white sesame seeds

1 small red onion, chopped

¼ cup dried cranberries

1 recipe Simple Lemon-Tahini Dipping Sauce (page 181)

Cooling Cucumber Salad with Roasted Chickpeas, page 69, Raw Broccoli Tahini Salad, page 113, Sweet Coconut Brown Rice and Gungo Peas, page 97, and Toby's Cuban Lime-Soaked Chicken, page 93

# Healthy Sweet Potato "Cheesy" Fries

The benefits of sweet potatoes are endless, and I love them prepared this way. The nutritional yeast gives them a cheesy taste that kids and adults love. Serve them with the Callaloo, Pumpkin, and Lentil Burgers (page 84) or Spicy Mahi-Mahi Fish Burgers (page 98).

| YIELD: 2 servings | PREP TIME: 15 minutes | COOK TIME: 25 minutes |
|---|---|---|

## PROCEDURE

1. Preheat the oven to 475°F. Lightly coat a baking sheet with olive oil, or line with parchment paper.

2. In a small bowl, combine the nutritional yeast, garlic, onion powder, and cayenne. Season to taste with salt and pepper.

3. Add the 3 tablespoons of olive oil and whisk until combined.

4. Pour the spice mixture into a large resealable plastic bag. Add the sweet potatoes and shake to coat them with the oil mixture.

5. Arrange the sweet potatoes in a single layer on the baking sheet. Make sure they are not "overcrowded"—use two pans if necessary. Bake for 15 minutes. Flip the fries over and cook for another 10 minutes, until tender and golden brown.

6. Remove from the oven and enjoy with your favorite dipping sauce.

## INGREDIENTS

3 tablespoons extra-virgin olive oil, plus more for the baking sheet

2 tablespoons nutritional yeast

1 clove garlic, minced

1 teaspoon onion powder

1 pinch cayenne pepper

Himalayan sea salt

Ground black pepper

2 medium sweet potatoes, cut into ¼-inch strips

# Snack Time

*Gluten-Free Vegan Superfood Snacks
and Appetizers to Rock Your World*

When I discovered that I had an allergy to wheat, a whole new world opened up for me. I got into my kitchen with Miss Neng and we played and experimented for months with different recipes. Here are the recipes that worked and are now part of our line of gluten-free vegan superfood snacks. Not only are they simple to make, they contain superfoods to fuel your day and help you to live life to its fullest. Make them, freeze them, and always share them!

Dr. Tracey's Herbed Seed Bread, page 127

# Herbed Avocado Hummus

There are so many versions of hummus to choose from, but this one, with its savory combination of avocado and fresh herbs from the garden, is my favorite. This hummus is the perfect superfood snack as it's packed with slow-digesting carbs, belly-filling fiber, cholesterol-lowering avocado, and hunger-deflecting protein.

| YIELD: 2½ cups | PREP TIME: 15 minutes + overnight soaking if using dried chickpeas | COOK TIME: 90 minutes if using dried chickpeas |
| --- | --- | --- |

## PROCEDURE

1. If you are using dried chickpeas, soak them overnight in a medium pot of water. Drain the water and rinse the chickpeas before cooking. If using canned chickpeas, skip to Step 4.

2. Place the chickpeas in a large pot and cover with several inches of water. I use about 1 cup of soaked beans to 1 quart of water. Bring to a boil, then reduce to a simmer for 75 to 90 minutes, until they are tender yet firm.

3. Leave the beans to cool.

4. Using the cooled chickpeas or the canned version, blend the chickpeas with all the remaining ingredients in a food processor or high-speed blender until smooth, about 5 minutes.

5. Add additional water if the hummus is too thick. Season with salt as needed.

6. Serve with Savory Flaxseed Crackers (page 131) or Dr. Tracey's Herbed Seed Bread (page 127).

7. Store in an airtight container in the refrigerator for 3 to 5 days.

## INGREDIENTS

- 1 (15-ounce) can chickpeas, drained and rinsed or 1 cup dried chickpeas
- ¼ cup fresh lemon juice
- ¼ cup water, plus more as needed
- 3 tablespoons tahini
- 2 cloves garlic
- ⅓ cup diced avocado
- 2 tablespoons finely chopped fresh cilantro, or 2 teaspoons ground coriander
- 1 tablespoon finely chopped fresh thyme, or 1 teaspoon dried
- 2 tablespoons finely chopped fresh parsley, or 2 teaspoons dried
- 1 sliver Scotch bonnet or habanero pepper, seeded
- 1 tablespoon nutritional yeast
- ¼ teaspoon ground cumin
- ¼ teaspoon Himalayan sea salt, plus more as needed

# Franny's Blessed Hummus

My beautiful sister-in-law Franny Mahfood is not only a friend, but also one of the most respected nutritionists in Jamaica and the creator of The Right Weigh. When you visit her house, you are guaranteed to be greeted with a warm hug, laugh your head off at her jokes, and eat her Blessed Hummus with some olives and za'atar bread.

| YIELD: 2 cups | PREP TIME: 15 minutes + overnight soaking if using dried chickpeas | COOK TIME: 90 minutes if using dried chickpeas |
|---|---|---|

## PROCEDURE

1. If you are using dried chickpeas, soak them overnight in a medium pot of water. Drain the water and rinse the chickpeas before cooking. If using canned chickpeas, skip to Step 4.

2. Place the chickpeas in a large pot and cover with several inches of water. I use about 1 cup of soaked beans to 1 quart of water. Bring to a boil, then reduce to a simmer for 75 to 90 minutes, until they are tender but firm.

3. Leave beans to cool.

4. Using the cooled chickpeas or the canned version, blend the chickpeas and the garlic, Scotch bonnet to taste, lime juice, tahini, olive oil, salt, and water in a high-speed blender or food processor until smooth, about 5 minutes.

5. If the hummus is too thick, drizzle cold water into the blender and blend until smooth.

6. Garnish with the parsley, olive oil, and paprika.

7. Serve with Savory Flaxseed Crackers (page 131) or Dr. Tracey's Herbed Seed Bread (page 127).

8. Be like Fran: give a hug and make everyone laugh—it makes everything taste better!

## INGREDIENTS

1 (15-ounce) can chickpeas, drained and rinsed or 1 cup dried chickpeas

2 cloves garlic

Scotch bonnet or habanero pepper, minced (optional)

½ cup fresh lime juice

4 tablespoons tahini

2 tablespoons extra-virgin olive oil, plus more for garnish

1 teaspoon Himalayan sea salt

Cold water, as needed

Handful chopped parsley, for garnish

Paprika, for garnish

# Holy Holy Guacamole

When avocados (or pear, as we call them in Jamaica) are ripe, we make guacamole! Healthy fats are key to a healthy life. Eating them nourishes the skin; enhances the absorption of fat-soluble vitamins, minerals, and other nutrients; and may even help boost the immune system.

| YIELD: 3 cups | PREP TIME: 15 minutes |
|---|---|

## PROCEDURE

1.  In a medium bowl, roughly mash the avocado using a fork. (Don't overdo it! The guacamole should be a little chunky.)

2.  Add the salt, lemon juice, onions, cilantro, black pepper to taste, and Scotch bonnet to taste.

3.  Cover with plastic wrap and chill to prevent air reaching the guacamole. (The oxygen in the air causes oxidation, which will turn the guacamole brown.)

4.  Refrigerate (for no more than 24 to 36 hours) and add the tomatoes when you're ready to serve.

5.  This is the perfect high-vitality appetizer when served with Savory Flaxseed Crackers (page 131) or Dr. Tracey's Herbed Seed Bread (page 127).

## INGREDIENTS

2 large ripe avocados, diced

½ teaspoon Himalayan sea salt

2 tablespoons fresh lemon or lime juice

2 tablespoons minced red onion

2 tablespoons finely chopped fresh cilantro

Ground black pepper

Scotch bonnet or habanero pepper, seeded and minced

1 large tomato, seeded and chopped

# Scotch Bonnet Cashew Cream Cheese

I love cheese, but in my detox programs we eliminate all forms of dairy. I had to find something that I could substitute and still give me that dairy satisfaction—this is it. A great mineral source, cashews contain zero cholesterol and are full of copper, magnesium, phosphorus, and vitamin K. Bye-bye, cream cheese!

---

YIELD: 1 cup

PREP TIME: 10 to 15 minutes
+ overnight soaking of the cashews

---

## PROCEDURE

1. In a small bowl of water, soak cashews overnight to soften.

2. Drain the cashews.

3. Blend the cashews with the ¼ cup water and the lime juice in a high-speed blender until smooth, about 1 to 2 minutes, stopping occasionally to scrape the mixture from the sides of the blender.

4. Transfer the mixture to a medium bowl and add the nutritional yeast, parsley, shallots, chives, salt, and Scotch bonnet. Stir well to combine.

5. Serve on Dr. Tracey's Herbed Seed Bread (page 127) or Savory Flaxseed Crackers (page 131). It's great as a dip for veggies too.

## INGREDIENTS

1 cup raw cashews

¼ cup water

1 tablespoon fresh lime or lemon juice

1 tablespoon nutritional yeast

1 tablespoon minced fresh parsley

1 tablespoon minced shallots

¼ cup minced chives

1 teaspoon Himalayan sea salt

1 sliver Scotch bonnet or habanero pepper, minced

# Jerked Almond Pâté

This recipe is inspired by my beautiful friend Chorvelle Johnson, author of *Simply Vegan: The Jamaican Way*. This has got to be the best pâté on the planet. Made with raw almonds and spiced with jerk seasoning, it's a gluten-free, vegan, high-protein, knock-your-socks-off delicious spread, dip, and sauce you can use on everything.

YIELD: 2½ cups

PREP TIME: 5 to 10 minutes +
2 to 3 hours to soak the almonds

## PROCEDURE

1. Fill a medium bowl with water and soak the almonds for 2 to 3 hours. Drain and remove the skin. (To do this, use your fingers to gently squeeze the almonds and loosen the skin from them; take care not to squeeze too hard or they'll shoot across the room, which is fun but not superpractical! Squeeze them from one hand into the other to keep them from "launching" too far.)

2. Put the almonds and all the remaining ingredients in a high-speed blender and puree till smooth, about 3 to 4 minutes.

3. Add a little more water if needed (it should be spreadable).

4. Serve over Dr. Tracey's Herbed Seed Bread (page 127), on Callaloo, Pumpkin, and Lentil Burgers (page 84), with Savory Flaxseed Crackers (page 131), or as a dip for anything!

5. This keeps in a glass container in the refrigerator for 3 to 5 days.

## INGREDIENTS

1½ cups raw almonds

3 cloves garlic, minced

1 medium onion, minced

2 whole scallions, chopped

¼ Scotch bonnet or habanero pepper, seeded and finely chopped

½ cup + 1 tablespoon water, plus more as needed

3 tablespoons fresh lemon juice

2 tablespoons coconut oil

1 tablespoon nutritional yeast

1 teaspoon Himalayan sea salt

# Dr. Tracey's Herbed Seed Bread

When searching for a gluten-free alternative to bread, my friend Dr. Tracey Wright gave me this wonderful recipe. There's nothing I love more for dinner than a bowl of Green Goddess Detox Soup (page 140) and a couple pieces of this bread with Herbed Avocado Hummus (page 119) or Jerked Almond Pâté (page 126).

| YIELD: 24 pieces | PREP TIME: 20 minutes | COOK TIME: 40 minutes |
| --- | --- | --- |

## PROCEDURE

1. Preheat the oven to 350°F. Rub a 9-by-13-inch baking pan with a little coconut oil, or use a nonstick baking pan.

2. In a large bowl, mix together the almond meal, almonds, pumpkin seeds, sunflower seeds, ground flaxseeds, walnuts, sesame seeds, nutritional yeast, garlic powder, rosemary, thyme, and salt.

3. Add the water and 2 tablespoons coconut oil and stir until the mixture is spreadable.

4. Spread the dough evenly in the prepared pan.

5. Cut into 24 squares.

6. Bake for 35 to 40 minutes, until golden brown.

7. Remove the bread carefully from the pan, cool, and store in an airtight container, where it will keep up to 1 week.

## INGREDIENTS

1 cup almond meal

½ cup sliced almonds

½ cup pumpkin seeds

½ cup sunflower seeds

½ cup ground flaxseeds

½ cup chopped walnuts

2 tablespoons sesame seeds

1 tablespoon nutritional yeast

1 tablespoon garlic powder

1 teaspoon finely chopped fresh rosemary

1 teaspoon finely chopped fresh thyme

½ teaspoon Himalayan sea salt

½ cup water

2 tablespoons coconut oil, plus more for the pan

# Sweet Seed Bread

Dr. Tracey taught me the savory version of this gluten-free bread, but one day I came up with this sweet seed bread. Any dried fruit works here; I like cranberries, dates, blueberries, and goji berries. Try it with some Homemade Sweet Cinnamon Almond Butter (page 161) for a filling, nutritious snack that will satisfy any sweet tooth.

| YIELD: 24 pieces | PREP TIME: 20 minutes | COOK TIME: 25 minutes |
|---|---|---|

## PROCEDURE

1. Preheat the oven to 350°F. Rub a 10-by-10-inch baking pan with a little coconut oil, or use a nonstick baking pan.

2. In a large bowl, mix together the almond meal, almonds, pumpkin seeds, sunflower seeds, ground flaxseeds, walnuts, dried fruit, sesame seeds, nutritional yeast, salt, and cinnamon.

3. Add the water, honey, and coconut oil and stir until the mixture is spreadable.

4. Spread the dough evenly in the prepared pan.

5. Cut into 24 squares.

6. Bake for 20 to 25 minutes, until golden brown.

7. Remove the bread carefully from pan, cool, and store in an airtight container, where it will keep for up to 1 week.

## INGREDIENTS

1 cup almond meal

½ cup sliced almonds

½ cup pumpkin seeds

½ cup sunflower seeds

½ cup ground flaxseeds

½ cup chopped walnuts

¼ cup finely chopped dried fruit

2 tablespoons sesame seeds

1 tablespoon nutritional yeast

¼ teaspoon Himalayan sea salt

½ teaspoon cinnamon

½ cup water

¼ cup honey or maple syrup

2 tablespoons coconut oil

# Cheesy Kale Chips

I was determined to get my kids off their chip addiction and this recipe did it! We always have an abundance of kale growing in the garden, so we make these chips instead of popcorn for movie nights. Full of protein and fiber, kale contains folate, a B vitamin that is key for brain development.

| YIELD: 2 to 4 servings | PREP TIME: 20 to 25 minutes | COOK TIME: 15 minutes |

## PROCEDURE

1. Preheat the oven to 350°F.

2. Remove and discard the tough stems from the kale. Tear the leaves into pieces and transfer them to a large bowl.

3. In a small bowl, combine the olive oil, nutritional yeast, salt, and pepper. Pour the mixture over the kale and massage it into the leaves.

4. Transfer the kale to a baking sheet and bake for 10 to 15 minutes, until crispy.

5. We usually eat these right away because they tend to get soggy, but you can store in an airtight container for 2 to 3 days.

## INGREDIENTS

1 pound kale

2 tablespoons extra-virgin olive oil

1 tablespoon nutritional yeast

½ teaspoon Himalayan sea salt

½ teaspoon ground black pepper

# Savory Flaxseed Crackers

OK, I'm just warning you: these crackers are addictive. They are savory; they are crunchy; they are gluten-free; they are filling; and they are so, so good for you. Try them with Jerked Almond Pâté (page 126), Holy Holy Guacamole (page 123), or Scotch Bonnet Cashew Cream Cheese (page 124). Snacking does not get better than this.

| YIELD: 24 crackers | PREP TIME: 10 minutes | COOK TIME: 35 minutes |
| --- | --- | --- |

## PROCEDURE

1. Preheat the oven to 350°F.

2. In a large bowl, mix together the ground flaxseeds, almond flour, brown rice flour, nutritional yeast, sesame seeds, garlic powder, rosemary, thyme, baking soda, and salt.

3. Add the water and coconut oil slowly, stirring continuously, and stir until moist and crumbly.

4. Immediately transfer the mixture to a 9-by-13-inch nonstick baking pan, flattening it with your fingertips.

5. Use a knife to cut into 24 squares.

6. Bake on the lower oven rack for 20 to 25 minutes, until the crackers are hard.

7. Move the baking sheet to the upper oven rack for 8 more minutes, or until the crackers are golden brown.

8. Remove from the oven and allow to cool.

9. Gently remove the crackers with a spatula.

10. Try not to eat the whole batch in one sitting. Store them in an airtight container if you don't eat them all immediately; they will keep for 5 to 7 days.

## INGREDIENTS

¼ cup ground flaxseeds

¾ cup almond flour

¾ cup brown rice flour

1 tablespoon nutritional yeast

1 tablespoon sesame seeds

1 tablespoon garlic powder

1 teaspoon chopped fresh rosemary

1 teaspoon chopped fresh thyme

1 teaspoon baking soda

½ teaspoon Himalayan sea salt

⅓ cup water

2 tablespoons coconut oil, melted

Herbed Avocado Hummus, page 119, and Savory Flaxseed Crackers, page 131

# Mahek's Indian Popcorn with Nutritional Yeast

My kids love popcorn, but almost all corn is genetically modified, and I try to keep them away from GMO foods such as wheat, soy, and corn. It's not always possible, but I do try! My dear friend Mahek, owner of the famous Nirvanna Indian restaurant in Kingston, gave me this awesome recipe for lotus seed "popcorn." Lotus seeds, also known as *phool makhana*, are readily available in Indian grocery stores and are not only low in calories, but also high in magnesium. They also contain a powerful antiaging enzyme. Movie nights are never going to be the same!

| YIELD: 2 cups | PREP TIME: 5 minutes | COOK TIME: 5 minutes |
| --- | --- | --- |

## PROCEDURE

1. Put all the ingredients in a large frying pan set over medium heat.

2. Stir for 3 to 5 minutes, until golden brown.

3. Serve hot and enjoy.

## INGREDIENTS

2 cups popped lotus seeds

1 tablespoon extra-virgin olive oil

1 tablespoon nutritional yeast

1 pinch Himalayan sea salt

1 pinch ground black pepper

## SIX TIPS FOR STARTING YOUR VERY OWN ORGANIC GARDEN

My family grows a little organic garden each year, where we plant our own greens, tomatoes, and more. I can't express enough how much joy it has given my family and me. Planting the seeds, watering, weeding, and patiently waiting for the tomatoes or okra or callaloo to bear fruit—it's all something that we share. There is also great comfort in knowing that what we pick is pesticide- and fertilizer-free. Our produce is fresh, close to the source, and 100 percent organic. You can absolutely taste the difference!

Not everything grows perfectly and I'm still learning. I'm also very blessed to have an experienced gardener, my dear friend Lass, who comes once a week to check things out. Lass too has learned so much and is now growing kale for his community.

If you want to start your own organic garden, here are my six simple steps.

### 1. Start Small

You don't need a farm! I live in a townhouse complex in Montego Bay with just a tiny bit of land in front. Instead of planting flowers, I decided I wanted an organic garden. My mom thought I was crazy, but I did it anyway.

### 2. Grow in Boxes

When I built my garden I consulted my amazing friend and organic grower extraordinaire Liz Sloms to give me some tips. She advised getting three (four-by-six-foot) cedar boxes built instead of planting in the ground. Not only do the boxes look neat and nice in my small space, but the garden is also much easier to take care of this way, as the soil is contained. Please use cedar to build your boxes; it helps to keep away the bugs and can stand the elements. Be sure to keep enough space between the boxes so you can walk around to water and weed.

### 3. Use Organic Soil

To get the best results from your new organic garden, make sure your soil is properly conditioned. Plants have to eat too, so make sure your veggies get lots of fresh nutrients. It's a great idea to invest in organic, nutrient-rich soil from an agricultural store.

### 4. Know What You Grow

I decided to start with growing things I know we use often in our home. Our first seeds were callaloo, tomato, cabbage, lettuce, and bok choy. Now that we are getting brave, we're experimenting with all kinds of peas, kale, broccoli, mixed greens, and fancy lettuces. It is so exciting! Just know that no matter what you choose to grow, you are going to win some and lose some.

### 5. Keep the Bugs at Bay

This can be challenging! Nothing is more disheartening than waking up to find your latest crop eaten overnight. One of the tricks I learned is to plant lemongrass all around my garden beds. This has really helped. You may not be able to grow lemongrass in your climate, so try this tip: spray a mixture of boiled garlic and Scotch bonnet on the plants if you see bugs.

### 6. Water, Water, Water

It's so hot in Montego Bay that I water both morning and evening, but the best time is in the morning when the air is cool. If you are going to be away, be sure to ask someone to water for you.

**Most of all, I encourage you to have fun with it!** You are going to love being able to pick your own greens for your morning shake or lunchtime salads. Also, as I'm sure some of you are aware, buying organic is not cheap. Growing your own garden is an amazing way to save some money on your high-vitality life!

Pumpkin Coconut-Ginger Soup, page 142

# Dinnertime

## *High-Vitality Soups That Are Filling and Nutritious*

One of the principles of my seven-day Live Fit Detox Program is giving the digestive system twelve good hours of rest between the last meal at night and breakfast the next morning. Your digestive system needs that time to do its job of digestion, absorption, and assimilation. Even if you're not doing a detox program, you can still benefit from a detox dinner: supernutritious soup with a delicious salad. The soup recipes in this section are creative to ensure that they are not only full of nutrition, but are alkalizing and filling as well. Foods that produce more acidic residues have come to be deemed potentially harmful and disease producing, while alkaline foods are deemed potentially healthier—so we want to eat alkalizing foods, especially at dinnertime. Like a smoothie, the wealth of ingredients in a bowl of soup provides a good balance of carbohydrates, protein, and fats as well as the vitamins and minerals from veggies. Most nights, unless we're going out for dinner, my husband and I enjoy one of these soups and a great salad. We find that eating light at night helps us to sleep better and gives us more energy in the morning. We love it! Also, all these soups freeze beautifully. I recommend making a big batch and freezing what you don't eat right away, so that soup is always an option at the end of a long day.

# Green Goddess Detox Soup

One evening when I was enjoying my Green Goddess Detox Soup, my son Elias said, "OMG, Mom, that soup is so alive it looks like it is breathing!" Well, he totally got it. That's what I want to put into my body and what I want you to put into yours too: food that is alive and makes you feel alive. And yes, food that tastes delicious too. Make this soup with spinach, broccoli, kale, or string beans if you don't have zucchini. It's simple, superalkalizing, and delicious, and your digestive system will love you for it.

| YIELD: 4 (2-cup) servings | PREP TIME: 20 minutes | COOK TIME: 20 minutes |
| --- | --- | --- |

## PROCEDURE

1. Heat a large, deep sauté pan over medium heat for 2 to 3 minutes. Add the coconut oil and swirl to evenly coat the pan.

2. Sauté the garlic, onions, thyme, scallions, and celery for 5 minutes, until the celery and onions are tender.

3. Add the coconut milk plus 2 cups of water and bring to a boil for 5 minutes.

4. Add the zucchini, nutritional yeast, Scotch bonnet, and salt. Season to taste with black pepper.

5. Remove from the heat and cool.

6. In batches, transfer the soup to a high-speed blender and blend until smooth.

7. Return the soup to the pan and cook over medium-low heat for 8 to 10 minutes, until hot.

8. Serve hot with Baked Coconut-Infused Bammy Chips or Croutons (page 168) or Roasted Chickpeas Crunch (page 169).

## INGREDIENTS

2 tablespoons coconut oil

1 clove garlic, minced

1 large onion, chopped

2 tablespoons chopped fresh thyme, or 2 teaspoons dried

2 whole scallions, chopped

2 stalks celery, chopped

3 cups Homemade Coconut Milk (page 159) or store-bought unsweetened coconut milk

2 to 4 cups water

3 pounds zucchini, sliced

2 tablespoons nutritional yeast

1 sliver Scotch bonnet or habanero pepper, seeded and minced

1 ½ teaspoons Himalayan sea salt

Ground black pepper

# Pumpkin Coconut-Ginger Soup

There is nothing better than a Jamaican pumpkin soup. This creamy, yummy-for-your-tummy soup is full of beta-carotene, which can strengthen your immune system, and island spices add a nice zip. We eat this soup at least once a week at home.

| YIELD: 4 (2-cup) servings | PREP TIME: 30 to 35 minutes | COOK TIME: 60 minutes |
| --- | --- | --- |

## PROCEDURE

1. Heat a large, deep frying pan over medium heat for 2 to 3 minutes. Add the coconut oil and swirl to evenly coat the pan.

2. Sauté the onions for 13 to 15 minutes, until golden brown, then add the garlic, ginger, scallions, and thyme. Cook for 5 minutes more.

3. Add the coconut milk, plus 2 cups of water. Bring to a boil.

4. Stir in the pumpkin, coriander, cumin, curry powder, and Scotch bonnet to taste. Cook until the pumpkin is soft, 25 to 30 minutes.

5. Season with the salt and pepper, remove from the heat, and let cool.

6. In batches, blend the soup and the nutritional yeast in a high-speed blender until smooth, adding more water if necessary.

7. Return the soup to the pan and cook over medium-low heat for 8 to 10 minutes, until hot.

8. Garnish with the additional scallions and serve.

## INGREDIENTS

2 tablespoons coconut oil

1 medium onion, chopped

4 cloves garlic, chopped

1 (3-inch) knob ginger, peeled and chopped

2 whole scallions, chopped, plus more for garnish

2 tablespoons chopped fresh thyme, or 2 teaspoons dried

2 cups Homemade Coconut Milk (page 159) or store-bought unsweetened coconut milk

2 to 4 cups water, plus more as needed

3 pounds pumpkin or butternut squash, diced

1 teaspoon ground coriander

1 teaspoon ground cumin

1 teaspoon curry powder

Scotch bonnet or habanero pepper, seeded and minced

1 teaspoon Himalayan sea salt

Ground black pepper

2 tablespoons nutritional yeast

# Curried Mung Bean Soup

Here are my mung beans again. I just love this soup. Filling, full of protein, and redolent of exotic Indian spices, this soup is a perfect meal.

| YIELD: 3 (2-cup) servings | PREP TIME: 15 minutes + overnight soaking of the mung beans | COOK TIME: 30 minutes |
| --- | --- | --- |

## PROCEDURE

1. Soak the mung beans overnight in a medium pot of water.

2. The next day, heat a large sauté pan over medium heat for 2 to 3 minutes. Add the coconut oil and swirl to evenly coat the pan.

3. Sauté the onions, garlic, thyme, scallions, and curry powder until the onions are lightly browned.

4. Rinse and drain the mung beans, then put them in a large pot. Add the coconut milk plus 2 cups water, bring to a boil, then turn down the heat and let simmer.

5. Cook for about 20 minutes, until the beans are tender, adding more water if they are too thick.

6. Add the carrots, celery, string beans, and nutritional yeast and cook for 10 minutes.

7. Remove the soup from the heat and add the onion mixture and the bok choy leaves. Serve hot.

## INGREDIENTS

2 cups mung beans

2 tablespoons coconut oil

1 medium onion, chopped

3 cloves garlic, minced

1 tablespoon chopped fresh thyme

2 whole scallions, chopped

1 teaspoon Indian curry powder

1 cup Homemade Coconut Milk (page 159) or store-bought unsweetened coconut milk

2 to 4 cups water, plus more as needed

1 medium carrot, diced

2 stalks celery, chopped

½ cup chopped string beans

1 tablespoon nutritional yeast

8 to 10 bok choy leaves, chopped

# Mediterranean Detox Veggie Soup

Sometimes I crave something superclean and simple. This light but filling soup is inspired by one of my favorite blogs, the *Mediterranean Dish* by Suzy Karadsheh, and is perfect for detox. Thanks, Suzy! If you want a little more body, add a can of whole peeled tomatoes. I love it just the way it is. Serve with Savory Flaxseed Crackers (page 131) and Herbed Avocado Hummus (page 119) for a delicious, healthy dinner.

**YIELD:** 5 (2-cup) servings     **PREP TIME:** 15 minutes     **COOK TIME:** 45 minutes

## PROCEDURE

1. In a large pot, heat 1 tablespoon olive oil over medium-high heat. Add the mushrooms and cook for 3 to 4 minutes, stirring regularly. Remove the mushrooms from the pot.

2. To the same pot, add the zucchini. Cook for 5 minutes, or until the zucchini begin to gain color, stirring regularly. Remove the zucchini from the pot.

3. Add the remaining 2 tablespoons olive oil to the pot and add the parsley, onions, garlic, celery, carrots, and sweet potatoes. Stir in the coriander, turmeric, paprika, thyme, and salt and pepper to taste.

4. Cook for 5 to 7 minutes, stirring regularly, until the vegetables have softened a bit.

5. Add the bay leaves and broth. Bring to a boil, then turn the heat down to medium. Cover and cook for 15 minutes.

6. Add the chickpeas and the sautéed mushrooms and zucchini. Cook for just a few more minutes, until everything is warmed through.

7. Stir in the lemon juice and zest.

8. Remove from the heat. Transfer to serving bowls and top with the toasted pine nuts.

## INGREDIENTS

3 tablespoons extra-virgin olive oil, divided

1 cup sliced fresh shiitake, oyster, or button mushrooms

2 medium zucchini, sliced into half-moons

1 bunch fresh parsley, chopped

1 medium onion, chopped

2 cloves garlic, chopped

2 stalks celery, chopped

2 medium carrots, chopped

2 sweet potatoes, diced

1 teaspoon ground coriander

½ teaspoon ground turmeric

½ teaspoon paprika

½ teaspoon chopped fresh thyme

Himalayan sea salt

Ground black pepper

2 bay leaves

6 cups low-sodium chicken or vegetable broth

2 cups cooked chickpeas, or 1 can, rinsed and drained

Juice and zest of 1 lemon

¼ cup pine nuts, toasted, for garnish

# Thai Coconut Curry Soup
# with Brown Rice Noodles

This is a soup to live for: you feel like you're in heaven when you eat it. I'm not sure if it's the fresh lemongrass, the homemade coconut milk, or the delicate brown rice noodles, but this soup is amazing! Add organic chicken or fresh fish if you want to make it a little heartier.

| YIELD: 5 (2-cup) servings | PREP TIME: 30 to 35 minutes | COOK TIME: 20 minutes |
| --- | --- | --- |

## PROCEDURE

1. Heat a large pot over medium heat for 2 to 3 minutes. Add the coconut oil and swirl to evenly coat the bottom of the pot.

2. Sauté the garlic, ginger, and scallions for 2 minutes.

3. Add the red curry sauce and stir for a few minutes, until everything sizzles.

4. Add the coconut milk plus 2 cups of water and bring to a boil.

5. Add the carrots, celery, lemongrass, nutritional yeast, and fish sauce and continue boiling for another 2 minutes.

6. Add the sprouted mung beans and brown rice noodles. Gently submerge them in the broth.

7. Turn off the heat and let stand until the noodles soften, 8 to 12 minutes.

8. Remove the lemongrass stalks and add more water if the soup is too thick.

9. Stir in the cilantro and lemon juice.

10. Taste and season with salt and pepper as needed.

11. Ladle the soup into a big bowl and garnish with the remaining scallions and cilantro.

## INGREDIENTS

2 tablespoons coconut oil

3 cloves garlic, minced

1 tablespoon grated ginger

2 whole medium scallions, chopped, some set aside for garnish

1 heaping tablespoon Thai red curry simmer sauce

4 cups Homemade Coconut Milk (page 159) or 2 cups store-bought unsweetened coconut milk

2 to 4 cups water, plus more as needed

2 large carrots, shredded

2 stalks celery, chopped

3 stalks lemongrass

2 tablespoons nutritional yeast

2 tablespoons fish sauce

2 cups Sprouted Mung Beans (page 167, optional)

4 ounces uncooked brown rice noodles

1 cup finely chopped fresh cilantro, some set aside for garnish

2 tablespoons fresh lemon or lime juice

Himalayan sea salt

Ground black pepper

# Spicy Lentil and Greens Soup

My husband loves this soup because it's filling and flavorful. Lentils are an excellent source of protein and iron and help to reduce cholesterol due to their high fiber content. High cholesterol runs in his family, so I do everything I can to make sure he gets lots of fiber each day.

| YIELD: 4 (2-cup) servings | PREP TIME: 1 hour | COOK TIME: 35 minutes |
| --- | --- | --- |

## PROCEDURE

1. Rinse the lentils and put them in a large pot. Soak them in 4 cups of water for one hour.

2. Drain and rinse the lentils, and cover them with fresh water. Bring the lentils to a boil and cook for 20 minutes, until the lentils are tender.

3. While the lentils are cooking, heat a large sauté pan for 2 to 3 minutes over medium heat. Add the coconut oil and swirl to evenly coat the pan.

4. Sauté the onions and garlic for 3 to 5 minutes, until golden brown, then add the carrots and tomatoes and cook for a few more minutes.

5. Add this mixture to the lentils.

6. Add the coconut milk plus 4 cups of water. Then add the celery, salt, Scotch bonnet, nutritional yeast, and thyme and continue cooking for 15 minutes.

7. Stir in the spinach and lemon juice.

8. To serve, ladle into bowls and garnish with the celery leaves and black pepper to taste.

## INGREDIENTS

14 ounces dried lentils

7 to 8 cups water, divided

1 tablespoon coconut oil

1 medium onion, chopped

4 cloves garlic, minced

1 medium carrot, chopped

1 large tomato, chopped

5 cups Homemade Coconut Milk (page 159) or store-bought unsweetened coconut milk

3 stalks celery, chopped

1 tablespoon Himalayan sea salt

¼ Scotch bonnet or habanero pepper, minced

1 tablespoon nutritional yeast

2 tablespoons chopped fresh thyme, or 2 teaspoons dried

2 cups baby spinach, kale, or callaloo

3 tablespoons fresh lemon juice

Celery leaves, for garnish

Ground black pepper

# Vegetarian Pepper Pot Soup with Yams and Green Bananas

Traditional Jamaican pepper pot soup dates back to the Taino, the original inhabitants of the Caribbean, and contains pork and some other ingredients I wouldn't describe as high-vitality foods. Here it's recreated with callaloo and yummy yams and green bananas. It is so good you'll be going back to the pot for more!

| YIELD: 4 (2-cup) servings | PREP TIME: 30 minutes | COOK TIME: 30 minutes |
|---|---|---|

## PROCEDURE

1. In a medium pot, bring the water, callaloo and coconut milk to a simmer over medium heat. Add salt to taste and simmer for 7 to 10 minutes, until the callaloo is tender.

2. Transfer the mixture to a high-speed blender and blend until smooth. Put it back into the pot.

3. Heat a large sauté pan over medium heat for 2 to 3 minutes. Add the coconut oil and swirl to evenly coat the pan.

4. Sauté the green bananas, carrot, Scotch bonnet, yams, thyme, scallions, and onions for 8 to 10 minutes, until tender but not mushy.

5. Pour the sautéed ingredients into the pot of coconut milk and simmer for 10 to 12 minutes, until the mixture has a creamy consistency with chunks of tender green bananas and yellow yams. Add the ground black pepper and nutritional yeast.

6. Serve with Baked Coconut-Infused Bammy Chips or Croutons (page 168) for a true Jamaican dinner!

## INGREDIENTS

2 to 4 cups water

2 pounds callaloo or spinach, stems removed and leaves sliced into strips

2 cups Homemade Coconut Milk (page 159) or store-bought unsweetened coconut milk

Himalayan sea salt

2 tablespoons coconut oil

2 green bananas, sliced

1 large carrot, chopped

1 Scotch bonnet pepper, minced

1 yam, chopped

1 big stalk fresh thyme

3 whole scallions, chopped

1 medium onion, chopped

Ground black pepper

2 tablespoons nutritional yeast

## YAMS VERSUS SWEET POTATOES

Although similar, yams and sweet potatoes come from different plant species. Similar in size and shape to sweet potatoes, yams have a higher sugar content and are not widely available in the United States (though sweet potatoes are sometimes mislabeled as yams). When in doubt, swap out sweet potatoes in recipes that call for yams.

# Fully Loaded Jamaican Pumpkin Chicken Soup

Sunday night dinner is always chicken soup and salad for our family. There is nothing like a Jamaican homemade chicken soup, full of delicious island spices. This soup is also deeply healing and comforting if you're not feeling well. Our kids love it and ask for it if they are coming down with something; they know that it's filled with goodness. This is the best recipe ever!

| YIELD: 4 (2-cup) servings | PREP TIME: 20 minutes | COOK TIME: 50 minutes |
| --- | --- | --- |

## PROCEDURE

1. In a large pot over medium-high heat, combine the water, pumpkin, garlic, onions, thyme, and scallions and bring to a boil. Boil for 20 minutes.

2. While this is boiling, heat a large frying pan over medium heat. Brown the chicken parts in the olive oil until golden brown.

3. Add the chicken and yellow yams to the soup and cook for 15 more minutes, until the chicken is cooked through.

4. Add the carrots, coconut milk, cauliflower, and nutritional yeast and cook for about 2 minutes, then add the broccoli and greens.

5. Remove from the heat so the greens and broccoli do not overcook.

6. Add the pimento cloves, bay leaves, and Scotch bonnet. Be mindful not to burst the pepper (or eat it for that matter). It's there for flavor!

7. Add the salt and pepper.

8. Return to the heat and simmer for another 10 minutes.

9. Remove the Scotch bonnet, serve, and savor the goodness!

## INGREDIENTS

5 cups water

2½ pounds diced pumpkin or butternut squash

3 cloves garlic, minced

1 medium onion, chopped

2 teaspoons chopped fresh thyme

2 whole scallions, chopped

2 pounds bone-in chicken parts, rinsed and dried

1 tablespoon extra-virgin olive oil

1 cup diced yellow yams

1 cup diced carrots

1 cup Homemade Coconut Milk (page 159) or store-bought unsweetened coconut milk

2 cups cauliflower, chopped

1 tablespoon nutritional yeast

2 cups broccoli, chopped

2 cups chopped greens (such as spinach or kale)

1 tablespoon pimento cloves (allspice berry)

2 bay leaves

1 whole Scotch bonnet or habanero pepper

1 teaspoon Himalayan sea salt

1 teaspoon ground black pepper

# Kale, Chicken, and Mushroom Soup

This recipe is inspired by mushroom grower and serial social entrepreneur Pauline Terri Smith, who recently moved back to Jamaica, the land of her birth, to help empower poor rural women to produce income by not only growing and selling mushrooms but also by learning how to use them in meal preparation for their families. I love how these flavors come together so beautifully, creating a warm, fuzzy feeling in my soul.

| YIELD: 4 (2-cup) servings | PREP TIME: 10 minutes | COOK TIME: 10 minutes |
| --- | --- | --- |

## PROCEDURE

1. Slice the chicken breast into long thin strips; season with the salt, pepper, nutritional yeast, and a drizzle of olive oil. Set aside.

2. In a large pot, heat the tablespoon of olive oil over medium heat. Stir-fry the light-green parts of the scallions until softened, about 1 minute.

3. Add the mushrooms and cook, stirring, until the mushrooms have softened, about 3 minutes. Season with salt.

4. Add the water and turn the heat to high. Bring the mixture to a boil; add the chicken strips and tamari. Gently stir and cook for 3 minutes.

5. Add more salt and pepper, if needed. Stir in the kale and remove from the heat.

6. Ladle the soup into individual bowls.

7. Serve with a drizzle of sesame oil and garnish with the dark-green parts of the scallions.

## INGREDIENTS

1 (10-ounce) boneless, skinless chicken breast

¼ teaspoon Himalayan sea salt, plus more as needed

⅛ teaspoon ground white pepper, plus more as needed

1 teaspoon nutritional yeast

1 tablespoon extra-virgin olive oil, plus more for drizzling

3 whole scallions, sliced (light- and dark-green parts separated)

8 ounces fresh oyster, shiitake, or button mushrooms, sliced

6 cups water

1 teaspoon wheat-free tamari

4 cups kale, stems removed and leaves coarsely chopped

Sesame oil

Homemade Vanilla Almond Milk, page 158

# All the Time

*Nut Milks, Nut Butters, Salad Dressings,*
*and Other Goodies You Should Have on Hand*
*All the Time for a High-Vitality Life*

In this section you will find a collection of recipes for nut milks, nut butters, salsas, tomato sauce, and salad dressings that you should always have on hand for a high-vitality life. If you're going to eat a plant-based diet, make sure you have amazing sauces and dressings. I'm a condiment queen. I love dipping sauces and dressings on everything, so it's really important for me that they are made with the highest quality ingredients. The recipes in this section are some of our family favorites.

As you will also see, I am nuts about nuts! I use nuts to make my own nut milks, nut butters, and toppings for my soups and salads. Besides being packed with plant-based protein, nuts contain high levels of healthy fats, vitamins, antioxidants, and fiber. They are great for cardiovascular health and increased longevity, and contrary to popular belief, eating healthy fats actually helps you lose weight. Far more often than not, if you're struggling with excess weight, it's because you're eating too much sugar and too many carbs. I truly believe a high-fat, moderate-protein, and low-carb diet is one of the most effective ways to shed stubborn weight; it helps shift your body from burning sugar to burning fat as its primary fuel. This kind of diet also promotes mitochondrial health, which is important for overall health and disease prevention. So bring on the nuts, baby!

# Homemade Vanilla Almond Milk

One of the best things I've ever done is learn to make my own almond milk. It's easy to make and simply delicious, and I don't think I could ever go back to regular milk or even store-bought almond milk, which is full of preservatives. Just be sure to buy a nut-milk bag (a fine-mesh fabric bag that you can strain your blended raw nut milk through) and make a little at a time as it only lasts about three days in the fridge. Most store-bought almond and other nut milks contain preservatives and additives, and don't taste half as good, so I use homemade almond milk in my lattes and teas, and of course with my Groovy Granola Cereal (page 41) for the perfect pre-Hour of Power breakfast!

YIELD: 2 cups       PREP TIME: 10 minutes active prep time
+ 3 to 4 hours soaking time

## PROCEDURE

1. In a medium bowl filled with water, soak the almonds for 3 to 4 hours, until the skins slough off easily with a gentle squeeze.

2. Rinse the skinned almonds very well in a strainer.

3. Place the almonds, water, dates, and vanilla in a high-speed blender and blend on high speed until smooth, about 3 to 4 minutes.

4. Pour the mixture through a piece of cheesecloth or nut-milk bag into a medium bowl.

5. Squeeze all the liquid out of the solids using your hands. Save all the lovely almond pulp in a resealable plastic bag in the freezer; use it to make Almond Bliss Balls (page 57) later.

6. Serve immediately or refrigerate for 3 to 4 days.

## INGREDIENTS

1 cup whole almonds

2 cups water

2 pitted dates

½ teaspoon vanilla extract

# Homemade Coconut Milk

I grew up in Jamaica with homemade coconut milk. It's easy to make and so rich and full of flavor. Miss Neng and I use only freshly made coconut milk in our soups and curries. I also love it with my Groovy Granola Cereal (page 41), and it's divine in my Morning Macachino (page 189) or Glorious Golden Milk (page 192). The milk is creamy, delicious, and so good for you. When preparing coconut milk for soup, I like to use more water so it is not as concentrated.

| YIELD: 1 cup | PREP TIME: 10 to 15 minutes |
|---|---|

## PROCEDURE

1. Blend the coconut and the water in a high-speed blender for 3 to 5 minutes, until the coconut is pureed.

2. Pour it through a nut-milk bag into a medium bowl. Squeeze all the liquid out of the solids with your hands.

3. Store in an airtight container in the fridge for 3 to 5 days.

## INGREDIENTS

1 cup of chopped dry coconut

1 cup water

# Homemade Sweet Cinnamon Almond Butter

I have a secret to tell you: this almond butter is my weakness. Like, I have to hide the almond butter from myself or I'll eat the whole jar in one go. This is hands-down the best almond butter recipe ever, and I'm pretty sure you will be hiding that jar from yourself too.

| YIELD: 2½ cups | PREP TIME: 20 minutes | COOK TIME: 10 minutes |
|---|---|---|

## PROCEDURE

1. Preheat the oven to 325°F.

2. Put the almonds on a baking sheet. Toast for 10 minutes. Let cool.

3. Pour the almonds into a food processor and process for 3 minutes, until the almonds look dry and mealy.

4. Add the salt, sugar, and cinnamon and continue processing for another 5 minutes, until the mixture is smooth and creamy. If you prefer a chunkier almond butter, process for 3 minutes, instead of 5.

5. Store in an airtight glass jar or other airtight container up to 4 weeks.

## INGREDIENTS

3 cups whole almonds

¾ teaspoon Himalayan sea salt

2 tablespoons brown sugar

1 teaspoon cinnamon

# Kid-Friendly Superfood Roasted Tomato Sauce

This tomato sauce is a staple in my home. We make it in batches and freeze it so we can put together a delicious pizza or pasta in minutes. I make it from market-fresh tomatoes, herbs from the garden (herbs from your local farmers market are great too), and tons of garlic. Everyone in the house loves it! It replaces ketchup and transforms into a gorgeous tomato soup. Or spread it on a gluten-free wrap, add some fresh mozzarella and grilled chicken, and you have a fantastic, healthy pizza. Don't forget tomatoes are an abundant source of lycopene, a potent antioxidant! This sauce is the bomb.

| YIELD: 4 cups | PREP TIME: 15 minutes | COOK TIME: 35 minutes |
| --- | --- | --- |

## PROCEDURE

1. Preheat a broiler to 350°F.

2. Place the tomatoes in a baking dish with the garlic, basil, and onions.

3. Pour the olive oil over the vegetables and mix together.

4. Place the baking dish under the broiler for 35 minutes, or until the tomatoes are roasted (cooked but still firm; skins will pop and begin to brown).

5. Allow the tomatoes to cool slightly, then pour the vegetables into a high-speed blender and add the Scotch bonnet to taste, the sugar and salt, and the black pepper to taste. Blend until smooth, about 3 to 4 minutes.

6. Pour the warm mixture over a bed of Italian Raw Pasta with Zucchini, Chocho, and Carrots (page 103), spread on a pizza base, or pour into a bowl and garnish with basil leaves for a delicious soup.

7. If you're not eating it right away, store the sauce in an airtight container and freeze for up to 4 weeks.

## INGREDIENTS

10 medium plummy (Roma) tomatoes, quartered

6 cloves garlic

¼ cup basil, chopped

1 medium onion, diced

¼ cup extra-virgin olive oil

Scotch bonnet or habanero pepper, seeded and minced

1 tablespoon brown sugar

1 teaspoon Himalayan sea salt

Ground black pepper

# Roasted Nuts and Seeds

I always, always have a mason jar full of Roasted Nuts and Seeds on hand in my kitchen. They are so easy to make and full of amazing nutrients such as magnesium, copper, protein, zinc, vitamins B and E, and healthy fats. Nuts are great for heart health and make everything taste yummy. Add a few dried fruits and some cacao nibs, and you have a Trail Mix ready to go.

| YIELD: 2 cups | PREP TIME: 15 minutes | COOK TIME: 5 minutes |
|---|---|---|

## PROCEDURE

1. Warm a medium skillet over low heat and add the almonds, pumpkin seeds, and sunflower seeds. Stir the nuts till they are slightly golden, about 4 minutes.

2. Remove from the heat, add the chia seeds and flaxseeds, and let cool.

3. Store in mason jars or resealable plastic bags for up to 1 week.

**NOTE:** Make Trail Mix by adding ¼ cup dried fruit, 1 tablespoon cacao nibs or chocolate chips, and a pinch of Himalayan sea salt to the Roasted Nuts and Seeds. Trail mix is a delicious healthy snack to take with you or to have for your kids on the road.

## INGREDIENTS

½ cup sliced almonds

½ cup pumpkin seeds

½ cup sunflower seeds

¼ cup chia seeds

¼ cup flaxseeds

# Sprouted Mung Beans

The mung bean, a small green legume found in the Chinese or Indian section of the supermarket, is known in Ayurveda as "one of the most cherished foods" due to its high protein, antioxidant, and fiber content. We love to sprout all kinds of beans in our house, but mung beans are our favorite. Crispy and nutty tasting, they are hardy enough to be cooked in stir-fries and soups, and used raw in salads and wraps. Get sprouting now—it's easy and fun!

YIELD: 2 cups                 PREP TIME: 2 days

## PROCEDURE

1. Rinse the beans thoroughly and place them in a wide container (such as a glass baking dish).

2. Add the water, cover with a paper towel, and leave in a cool spot for 48 hours, until the beans begin to sprout.

3. Once the beans have sprouted, rinse them with fresh water, allowing the skin to naturally float off the beans.

4. Drain all the water and keep the beans refrigerated in an airtight glass container lined with paper towel. They will keep 1 week.

5. Sprinkle the beans on your favorite salad or use in soup. We also love to toast ours with a little olive oil and Himalayan sea salt for a delicious superfood snack!

## INGREDIENTS

1 cup mung beans

2 cups water

# Baked Coconut-Infused Bammy Chips or Croutons

Bammy is traditional Jamaican cassava bread descended from the simple flatbread eaten by the Taino, Jamaica's original inhabitants. Today it's produced in many rural communities and sold in stores and by street vendors in Jamaica and abroad (purchase it on Amazon.com). Gluten-free and full of fiber, bammy makes a perfect high-quality carb. These simple-to-make bammy crackers are an amazing snack, and the bammy croutons are a perfect addition to salads or topping for soup.

**YIELD:** 24 chips or 2 cups croutons  **PREP TIME:** 35 minutes  **COOK TIME:** 15 minutes

## PROCEDURE

1. Cut bammy rounds into wedges with kitchen scissors. If you are making bammy croutons, cut them into small squares. Place the pieces in a shallow dish.

2. In a medium bowl, mix the coconut milk, salt, nutritional yeast, and garlic powder together and pour over the bammy. Let soak for 30 minutes.

3. Preheat the oven to 350°F.

4. Take the bammy out, shake off any liquid, and place the pieces in a single layer on a baking sheet.

5. Bake 10 to 15 minutes, until the bammy is golden brown.

6. Serve with Jerked Almond Pâté (page 126) or Herbed Avocado Hummus (page 119) instead of chips or on top of your soups for a gluten-free crunch.

7. Store in a resealable plastic bag for up to a week.

## INGREDIENTS

4 large, round, thin bammy

½ cup Homemade Coconut Milk (page 159) or store-bought unsweetened coconut milk

½ teaspoon Himalayan sea salt

2 tablespoons nutritional yeast

½ teaspoon garlic powder

# Roasted Chickpeas Crunch

I love anything spicy and crunchy, and these curried chickpeas
certainly are both. I make them every week and toss them on salads,
use them as a topping on soups, or eat them as a snack.

| YIELD: 4 cups | PREP TIME: 5 minutes + overnight soaking if using dried chickpeas | COOK TIME: 35 minutes + 90 minutes if using dried chickpeas |
| --- | --- | --- |

## PROCEDURE

1. If you are using dried chickpeas, soak them overnight in a large pot of water. Drain the water and rinse the chickpeas before cooking. Skip to Step 3 if you are using canned chickpeas.

2. Place the chickpeas in a large pot and cover with several inches of water. I use about 1 cup of soaked beans to 1 quart of water. Bring to a boil, and then reduce to a simmer for 75 to 90 minutes, until they are tender yet firm.

3. Preheat the oven to 350°F.

4. Place the chickpeas in a large bowl and toss with the remaining ingredients until evenly coated.

5. Spread the chickpeas in an even layer on a large rimmed baking sheet.

6. Bake for 30 to 35 minutes, until crispy.

7. Store in an airtight container for up to 1 week.

## INGREDIENTS

4 cups dried chickpeas or 2 (15-ounce) cans, drained and rinsed

4 tablespoons olive oil

1 teaspoon nutritional yeast

1 teaspoon ground cumin

1 teaspoon chili powder

½ teaspoon cayenne pepper

1 big pinch Himalayan sea salt

# Pineapple, Cilantro, and Scotch Bonnet Salsa

As you can tell, mi love mi peppa! I also adore pineapple and cilantro,
and this salsa on a piece of grilled fish or chicken is to live for.

---

YIELD: 2 cups                    PREP TIME: 5 to 10 minutes

---

## PROCEDURE

1.  In a medium bowl, mix together all the ingredients.
    Chill in the fridge for 2 hours before serving
    to allow the flavors to come together.

2.  Store in an airtight container for up to 3 days.

## INGREDIENTS

1 cup chopped pineapple

1 small red onion, chopped

2 medium tomatoes, chopped

¼ cup chopped fresh cilantro

¼ cup chopped fresh basil

½ Scotch bonnet or habanero
    pepper, finely chopped

1 teaspoon fresh lemon juice

1 teaspoon brown sugar

½ teaspoon Himalayan sea salt

# Pickled Beets with Pimento and Scotch Bonnet

A jar of pickled beets can always be found in our fridge. My family eats them with practically every meal, and we love this spicy version that has pimento berries (allspice) and Scotch bonnet peppers. Beets are high in vitamin C, fiber, and essential minerals—what's not to love?

| YIELD: 4 cups | PREP TIME: 45 minutes | COOK TIME: 30 minutes |
| --- | --- | --- |

## PROCEDURE

1. Remove the greens from the beets and discard or save to use later. Wash the beets thoroughly, scrubbing away any dirt.

2. Place the beets in a medium saucepan over medium-high heat, covering with about an inch of water. Bring to a boil, then simmer for 20 to 30 minutes, until you can pierce them easily with a fork.

3. Rinse the beets in cold water and use your fingers to remove the peels.

4. Quarter or slice the beets and place them in a large heat-proof glass jar.

5. In a small saucepan over medium-high heat, combine the vinegar, sugar, salt, and black pepper. Bring to a boil.

6. Pour the mixture over the beets.

7. Add the pimento berries, bay leaves, and Scotch bonnet for flavor. Be mindful not to pierce the scotch bonnet as it will make the beets way too hot!

8. Leave in the fridge for a few days to pickle. The beets will last for up to 3 months in the fridge.

9. Serve as a side dish for everything!

## INGREDIENTS

5 large beets

1 cup apple cider vinegar

¼ cup brown sugar

½ teaspoon Himalayan sea salt

½ teaspoon ground black pepper

1 tablespoon pimento berries (allspice)

2 bay leaves

1 whole Scotch bonnet or habanero pepper

# Miss Maritess's Achara

Achara is a pickled condiment made from unripe papaya and served with grilled foods in the Philippines, to aid digestion. I just love it! This recipe comes from Miss Maritess, a wonderful lady from the Philippines who often helps me with my detox programs. The anti-inflammatory properties of ginger and turmeric combined with fiber-rich papaya make it a perfect high-vitality condiment. We always have a jar in the fridge and love it with grilled chicken or fish.

| YIELD: 4 cups | PREP TIME: 30 minutes | COOK TIME: 5 minutes |
| --- | --- | --- |

## PROCEDURE

1. In a small saucepan, bring the water and vinegar to a boil. Boil for 2 minutes, then set aside to cool.

2. Squeeze the papaya with your hands or in a nut-milk bag to remove the juice. Discard the juice.

3. Combine the papaya, carrots, ginger, turmeric, thyme, sugar, pineapple juice, and salt in a large mixing bowl. Mix thoroughly to combine the flavors, then transfer to a glass container.

4. Pour the vinegar mixture over the papaya mixture.

5. Leave in the fridge for a few days to pickle. The achara will last for up to 3 months in the fridge.

6. Serve as a side dish for everything!

## INGREDIENTS

½ cup water

½ cup white vinegar

2 large green papaya, peeled, seeded, and grated

¼ cup shredded carrots

1 tablespoon finely chopped fresh ginger

1 tablespoon finely chopped fresh turmeric

2 teaspoons finely chopped fresh thyme

½ cup brown sugar

2 cups pineapple juice

1 teaspoon Himalayan sea salt

# Pineapple, Rosemary, and Ginger Dressing

I could drink this dressing! The flavors of pineapple, rosemary (often freshly picked from our organic garden), and ginger turn every salad into a party. This dressing is also delicious as a marinade for grilled chicken or as a dipping sauce for crudités in a pinch.

**YIELD:** 2 cups        **PREP TIME:** 3 to 5 minutes

## PROCEDURE

1. Put all the ingredients in a high-speed blender and blend until emulsified.

2. Pour into an airtight container and store in the fridge for up to 10 days.

## INGREDIENTS

1 cup diced pineapple

1 tablespoon chopped fresh ginger

1 tablespoon chopped fresh rosemary

½ cup extra-virgin olive oil

⅓ cup white balsamic vinegar or rice wine vinegar

2 tablespoons honey

1 pinch Himalayan sea salt

# Carrot-Ginger Zinger Dressing

What I love most about sushi restaurants is the carrot-ginger salad dressing most of them serve. Miss Neng and I came up with our own version, and I think we pretty much nailed it. Made with only the highest quality sesame oil (check your local health-food store) and organic carrots, this is as fresh as it gets.

**YIELD:** 2½ cups          **PREP TIME:** 3 to 5 minutes

## PROCEDURE

1. Put all the ingredients in a high-speed blender and blend until emulsified.

2. Toss with salad or use as a dipping sauce for vegetables.

3. Store in an airtight container in the refrigerator for up to a week.

## INGREDIENTS

2 large carrots, diced

1 tablespoon chopped fresh ginger

2 cloves garlic

¾ cup water

¼ cup rice wine vinegar

2 tablespoons sesame oil

1 tablespoon wheat-free tamari

1 tablespoon honey

⅛ teaspoon Himalayan sea salt

# Creamy Lemon, Cranberry, and Tahini Dressing

We wanted a yummy dipping sauce to go with our Spicy Mahi-Mahi Fish Burgers (page 98) and created this baby. It works as a tasty salad dressing too if you prefer a creamy dressing.

YIELD: 1¼ to 1½ cups          PREP TIME: 3 to 5 minutes

## PROCEDURE

1. Put all the ingredients in a high-speed blender and blend until emulsified.

2. Add more water and salt as needed.

3. Pour into an airtight container and store in the fridge for up to a week.

## INGREDIENTS

¼ cup dried cranberries

3 cloves garlic

1 cup water

⅓ cup fresh lemon juice

¼ cup extra-virgin olive oil

2 tablespoons honey

2 tablespoons tahini

½ teaspoon salt

# Simple Lemon-Tahini Dipping Sauce

This condiment is great as a dipping sauce for fish or lentil burgers, or as a sandwich spread instead of mayo.

YIELD: ½ cup                    PREP TIME: 10 minutes

## PROCEDURE

1. In a small bowl, whisk the lemon juice, tahini, honey, and Scotch bonnet together until well combined. Season to taste with salt and pepper.

2. Store in an airtight container in the refrigerator for up to a week.

## INGREDIENTS

3 tablespoons fresh lemon juice

1 tablespoon tahini

1 tablespoon honey

½ teaspoon minced Scotch bonnet or habanero pepper

Himalayan sea salt

Ground black pepper

# Lemony Pumpkin Seed Dressing

The pumpkin seed is a nutritional powerhouse wrapped up in a very small package. I love these seeds tossed over salads and sprinkled on soups, but I love them most in this dressing. It goes particularly well with kale and other hardy greens and can be used as a dip for roasted veggies. Yum!

| YIELD: 2 cups | PREP TIME: 20 minutes | COOK TIME: 15 minutes |
|---|---|---|

## PROCEDURE

1. Toast the pumpkin seeds in small dry skillet over medium-low heat until puffed but not brown, about 15 minutes.

2. Transfer the seeds to a plate to cool.

3. Put the seeds and the remaining ingredients in a high-speed blender and blend until emulsified.

4. Store in an airtight container in the refrigerator for up to 1 week.

## INGREDIENTS

½ cup pumpkin seeds

¼ cup chopped fresh cilantro

3 cloves garlic

1 cup water

½ cup extra-virgin olive oil

⅓ cup fresh lemon juice

1 tablespoon honey

1 teaspoon ground cumin

1 teaspoon Himalayan sea salt

# Asian Dipping Sauce for Everything

Made with wheat-free tamari instead of soy sauce, this perfectly designed dressing is a hit on my detox program. Soy sauce contains not only gluten, but also almost three hundred milligrams of sodium per teaspoon—so we've cut it out of our kitchen. Pour this sauce over chopped veggies as an exotic dressing, or use it for sushi or Jerk Chicken or Black Bean, Plantain, and Avocado Rice Wraps (page 88). Get ready to fall in love.

---

YIELD: ½ cup          PREP TIME: 10 to 15 minutes

---

## PROCEDURE

1. Mix the tamari, Scotch bonnet, vinegar, honey, ginger, and garlic in a small bowl.

2. Slowly drizzle in the sesame oil, whisking constantly until emulsified.

3. When the dressing is well combined, add the sesame seeds. Whisk again to incorporate them.

4. Serve immediately or refrigerate in an airtight container and use within 1 week.

## INGREDIENTS

4 tablespoons wheat-free, low-sodium tamari

1 teaspoon chopped Scotch bonnet or habanero pepper

1 tablespoon rice wine vinegar

1½ tablespoons honey

1½ tablespoons grated ginger

½ teaspoon minced garlic

1 tablespoon sesame oil

1 teaspoon black sesame seeds, lightly toasted

# Orange, Rosemary, and Honey
# Aged Balsamic Vinaigrette

It's simple, but when made with great olive oil and aged balsamic
vinegar, this everyday dressing can't be beat!

**YIELD:** 2 cups　　　　　**PREP TIME:** 15 minutes

## PROCEDURE

1. Blend all the ingredients together in a high-
   speed blender until emulsified, adding a little
   water or extra orange juice if needed.

2. Store in an airtight container in the
   refrigerator for up to 1 week.

## INGREDIENTS

Juice of 1 large orange, plus more as
needed

1 teaspoon finely chopped fresh
rosemary

4 cloves garlic, minced

½ cup aged balsamic vinegar

½ cup extra-virgin olive oil

2 tablespoons Dijon mustard

2 tablespoons honey

# Teatime

## *Healing Lattes, Teas, and Elixirs*

Anyone who knows me knows that one of the hardest things for me to give up during my detox programs is coffee. I'm a certified coffee addict! I have, however, elevated my coffee by drinking only organic coffee and using my Homemade Vanilla Almond Milk (page 158) instead of dairy. I also now stick to my rule of one cup per day (most of the time). This section contains not only the recipe for my Morning Macachino (page 189), but also the recipes for my favorite afternoon and bedtime teas, detox elixirs, and tonics that I use on a daily basis.

# Morning Macachino

This coffee recipe uses honey or coconut sugar instead of white sugar and gives your body a superfood energy charge with maca powder and your blood sugar balance with cinnamon. Your mornings will never be the same! This recipe is absolutely delicious and even good for you. So, my fellow coffee lovers, up the ante on your coffee habit: commit to one cup a day and enjoy it.

---

**YIELD:** 1 serving          **PREP TIME:** 5 minutes

---

## PROCEDURE

1. Put coffee, almond milk, maca powder, cinnamon, and honey to taste in a high-speed blender and blend until combined.

2. Serve hot or cold.

## INGREDIENTS

1 cup brewed coffee

⅛ cup Homemade Vanilla Almond Milk (page 158) or Homemade Coconut Milk (page 159) or store-bought unsweetened almond or coconut milk

1 teaspoon maca powder

1 pinch cinnamon

Honey or coconut sugar

# Matcha Mint Tea Latte

Matcha tea is made from handpicked chlorophyll-rich tea leaves that are ground into a fine green powder. One cup of matcha green tea has as many antioxidants as ten cups of regular tea! It's known to boost metabolism, increase energy, and fortify your immune system.

**YIELD:** 2 (1-cup) servings        **PREP TIME:** 10 minutes

## PROCEDURE

1. Place the mint leaves in a small saucepan, cover with the water, and bring to a boil. Strain out the mint leaves and let cool.

2. Transfer the mint tea to a high-speed blender. Add the matcha powder, honey, and almond milk to the mint tea and blend until combined.

3. Serve warm or iced. Decorate with a sprig of mint and enjoy!

## INGREDIENTS

- 1 cup fresh mint leaves, plus a sprig for garnish
- 2 cups water
- 2 teaspoons matcha tea powder
- 2 teaspoons honey
- ¼ cup Homemade Vanilla Almond Milk (page 158) or Homemade Coconut Milk (page 159) or store-bought unsweetened almond or coconut milk (optional)

# Glorious Golden Milk

I got this healing Ayurvedic recipe from my amazing yoga teacher, Rod Stryker.
If you have difficulty sleeping, this tea works wonders. Turmeric calms and
soothes inflammation and is also detoxifying for the liver and gallbladder.

| YIELD: 4 (1-cup) servings | PREP TIME: 5 minutes | COOK TIME: 10 minutes |
| --- | --- | --- |

## PROCEDURE

1. In a medium saucepan, bring the water, ginger, and turmeric to a boil. Boil for 10 minutes.

2. Strain and let cool.

3. Add the cinnamon, pepper, honey, and almond milk.

4. Transfer to a highspeed blender and blend until combined.

5. Serve warm or cold.

## INGREDIENTS

4 cups water

1 (3-inch) knob fresh ginger, peeled and grated, or 2 teaspoons ground

1 (3-inch) knob fresh turmeric, peeled and grated, or 2 teaspoons ground

1 teaspoon cinnamon

1 pinch ground black pepper

2 teaspoons honey

1 cup Homemade Vanilla Almond Milk (page 158) or Homemade Coconut Milk (page 159) or store-bought unsweetened almond or coconut milk

# Gentle Cleanse Detox Tea
# with Fennel, Cumin, and Coriander Seeds

Fresh and cleansing, this gentle tea aids in the detox process by speeding up digestion. It's great if you are feeling gassy or bloated.

YIELD: 1 (1-cup) serving          PREP TIME: 5 minutes

## PROCEDURE

1. Place all the seeds in the bottom of a mug and pour the hot water over them.

2. Allow the tea to brew for 3 minutes before drinking. You can strain the seeds if you wish, but I like to drink them with the tea.

## INGREDIENTS

1 teaspoon cumin seeds

1 teaspoon coriander seeds

1 teaspoon fennel seeds

1 cup hot water

Glorious Golden Milk, page 192, and Live Fit Detox Bars, page 52

Sunflower Seed–Cranberry Superfood Balls, page 59

# Old-Time Jamaican Cocoa Tea

This is a classic Jamaican version of hot chocolate. Made from all-natural ingredients, this high-vitality version will fill your heart and soul with so much joy.

YIELD: 4 (1-cup) servings or 2 (2-cup) servings | PREP TIME: 5 minutes | COOK TIME: 5 minutes

## PROCEDURE

1. Combine the water and milk in a medium saucepan.

2. Add the cacao powder, cinnamon, pimento berries, and nutmeg and bring to a boil. Boil, stirring frequently, for 5 minutes.

3. Lower the heat so the mixture simmers and stir in the salt and coconut sugar.

4. Remove the pimento berries.

5. Pour into mugs through a small strainer.

6. Sit, close your eyes, take a deep breath, have a sip, and feel that inner smile!

## INGREDIENTS

2 cups water

2 cups Homemade Vanilla Almond Milk (page 158) or Homemade Coconut Milk (page 159) or store-bought unsweetened almond or coconut milk

½ cup raw cacao powder

1 teaspoon cinnamon

4 pimento berries (allspice)

1 pinch ground nutmeg

1 pinch Himalayan sea salt

2 tablespoons coconut sugar or honey (optional)

# Turmeric, Ginger, and Lemongrass Anti-Inflammatory Elixir

I first tried this elixir in Bali and loved it so much that I incorporated it into my detox programs. I brew a large pot each week and keep it in my fridge so I always have it on hand. The anti-inflammatory, anticancer properties of ginger, turmeric, and lemongrass, along with liver-cleansing lemon, kidney-supporting cucumber, metabolism-boosting cinnamon, and cooling mint make a delicious, potent combination.

| YIELD: 16 cups | PREP TIME: 20 minutes | COOK TIME: 20 minutes |
| --- | --- | --- |

## PROCEDURE

1. In a large saucepan, bring the water to a boil.

2. Add the ginger, turmeric, lemongrass, cinnamon, and cayenne pepper. Boil for 20 minutes.

3. Allow the liquid to cool.

4. Strain the liquid and pour into mason jars or a jug.

5. To serve, add the sliced cucumbers, lemons, and mint sprigs. Serve hot with a teaspoon of honey for a delicious warm tea, or cold with sparkling water and ice for a refreshing drink.

6. Store in an airtight container in the refrigerator for up to a week.

## INGREDIENTS

2 quarts water

1 (3-inch) knob ginger, peeled and crushed

1 (3-inch) knob fresh turmeric, peeled and crushed

Handful lemongrass stalks

1 teaspoon cinnamon

1 pinch cayenne pepper

1 large cucumber, sliced

2 lemons or limes, sliced

3 sprigs fresh mint

# Immune-Boosting Tonic
# for Sore Throats and Coughs

My kids know that the minute they feel a sore throat or cough coming on, they need to come to Mummy for this tonic and a rest on the BioMat. Right away I make a fresh batch of this tonic, which is strong and fiery, and it works!

**YIELD:** 1 (4-ounce) serving          **PREP TIME:** 5 minutes

## PROCEDURE

1. Place all the ingredients in a high-speed blender and blend until smooth.

2. Strain and store in a glass jar in the fridge for up to a week.

3. Sip very slowly, adding more honey if necessary, or make into a tea by adding hot water to the mixture.

## INGREDIENTS

¼ cup fresh lemon or lime juice

3 teaspoons honey

1 tablespoon apple cider vinegar

1 teaspoon ground turmeric, or 1 (3-inch) knob fresh turmeric, grated

1 teaspoon ground ginger, or 1 (3-inch) knob fresh ginger, grated

1 pinch cinnamon

1 clove garlic

# Aloe Flush

I'm a huge believer in aloe. I have it growing all over my garden. I use it topically for sunburns and rashes and as a face mask. Once per week, without fail, I do an Aloe Flush. Not only does this drink help to alkalize the body, but it also does wonderful things for your digestive system and flushes all the junk in your colon. I don't need to say more—try it!

---

YIELD: 1 (6-ounce) serving          PREP TIME: 10 minutes

---

## PROCEDURE

1. Break a leaf off the aloe vera plant, as close to the stem as possible. To remove the skin, start by cutting off the spiky sides and the tough green outer leaf. You'll end up with just the translucent gel inside. Rinse the gel well to remove all the latex, which is the yellowish goo that can taste bitter and have a laxative effect if too much is consumed.

2. Put in a high-speed blender with the lemon juice and pineapple (or your favorite fruit).

3. Blend until smooth and drink just before you go to bed at night. Block your nose if you have to!

## INGREDIENTS

2 healthy stalks aloe vera leaf

1 tablespoon fresh lemon juice

¼ cup chopped pineapple or other fruit

# The 20 Percent!

*Sweet Treats with Recipes From*
*Family and Friends*

Remember the 80-10-10 rule that you follow 80 percent of the time? Well, these are my 20 percent recipes. That means that most of these recipes are not high-vitality or gluten-free or vegan or any of that good stuff; they are just damn delicious. If you're going to eat desserts, they better be the best! Some of these recipes were generously given to me by friends and family whom I love and adore. I hope you enjoy them.

# Raw Cacao Energy Bombs

Who doesn't love chocolate? I sure do, and I loved it even more when I found out that chocolate in its pure state is a superfood. Not only does it have more than three hundred nutritional compounds including magnesium, calcium, sulfur, zinc, iron, potassium, and copper, but it is also one of the richest sources of antioxidants on the planet! That's when I began experimenting with raw Jamaican cacao and came up with this recipe. Experiment with it; tailor yours to fulfill your chocolate obsession. Here is my favorite combo. Eating just one of these rich and yummy balls is as satisfying as eating a whole bar of chocolate.

| YIELD: 24 balls | PREP TIME: 20 minutes |
| --- | --- |

## PROCEDURE

1. Grind the almonds in a food processor or high-speed blender for 2 minutes, until finely ground.

2. Add the walnuts to the blended almonds, grind for just 2 more seconds, and transfer the nuts to a bowl.

3. Blend the dates and water in the food processor or blender, until smooth, about 4 to 5 minutes.

4. Scrape the dates into the bowl with the nuts.

5. Add the cocoa, cinnamon, salt, and vanilla to the bowl and use your hands (yes, it gets wonderfully messy) to mix everything together until the mixture is sticky.

6. Roll the mixture into bite-size balls.

7. Put the coconut in a small shallow bowl.

8. Dip each ball into the bowl of shredded coconut to make them pretty. (At Christmastime I like to get festive and roll them in ground goji berries or pistachio nuts.)

9. Don't eat all 24 balls at once! They are great gifts.

10. Store in an airtight container in the fridge or freezer, where they last up to three months.

## INGREDIENTS

1 cup whole almonds

½ cup whole walnuts,

1 cup pitted dates, chopped

½ cup water

1 cup raw cacao powder

½ teaspoon cinnamon

⅛ teaspoon Himalayan sea salt

1 tablespoon vanilla extract

¼ cup unsweetened shredded coconut, toasted

# Noa's No-Bake Oatmeal, Peanut Butter, and Chocolate Chip Squares

My youngest daughter, Noa, has been in the kitchen with me since she was a little girl. She's a certified foodie and even told us at age five that she's going to be a famous chef. You go, my Noa! Here is the recipe she wanted to share with you. It's so easy to make and because of this, it's a great way to get your young ones in the kitchen.

---

YIELD: 18 squares          PREP TIME: 15 minutes + 3 hours chill time

---

## PROCEDURE

1. Line an 8-by-8-inch baking dish with parchment paper.

2. In a medium bowl mix the peanut butter, maple syrup, and cinnamon until fully combined.

3. Add the oats and chocolate chips and use your hands to mix completely.

4. Press the mixture evenly into the baking dish.

5. Let sit in the fridge for 3 hours.

6. Cut into 18 squares.

7. Keep in the fridge in an airtight container for up to a week.

## INGREDIENTS

⅓ cup peanut butter

2 tablespoons maple syrup

1 teaspoon cinnamon

2 cups gluten-free old-fashioned oats

⅓ cup chocolate chips

# Mom's Carrot Cake with Cream Cheese Icing

I'm not a huge sugar fan, but when I do have it I go all the way. On my birthday, my beautiful mother always makes me this carrot cake, which I eat, savoring each bite and saving some for the next day's breakfast. This is truly the best carrot cake ever; it's packed with juicy carrots, and the cream cheese icing complements it beautifully. My mother always decorates this cake with hand-picked flowers from her garden. Thanks, Mama!

YIELD: 18 servings          PREP TIME: 1 hour          COOK TIME: 45 minutes

## PROCEDURE

1.  Preheat the oven to 350°F and butter a 9-by-13-inch pan.

2.  Combine all the ingredients in a large bowl. Using an electric mixer on medium speed, mix until well blended, about 4 to 5 minutes.

3.  Pour the batter into the prepared pan and bake for 45 minutes to an hour, until a toothpick inserted in the center comes out clean.

4.  Cool the cake completely before icing.

## INGREDIENTS

Butter, for greasing the pan

1 cup corn oil

3 large eggs

2 teaspoons vanilla extract

2 cups all-purpose flour

1 cup granulated sugar

2 teaspoons cinnamon

2 teaspoons baking soda

½ teaspoon Himalayan sea salt

2 cups shredded carrots

1 cup golden raisins

1 cup chopped walnuts

½ cup sweetened shredded coconut

½ cup crushed pineapple

1 recipe Cream Cheese Icing (recipe on opposite page)

## CREAM CHEESE ICING PROCEDURE

1. By hand or using an electric mixer on medium speed, cream the butter, cream cheese, and sugar until fluffy, about 5 minutes.

2. Stir in the pineapple and walnuts by hand.

3. Spread the icing on the cooled cake.

## INGREDIENTS

1 stick butter, softened

3 ounces cream cheese, softened

1½ cups powdered sugar

½ cup crushed pineapple

¼ cup chopped walnuts

# Fully Loaded Superfood Cookies

If you are looking for a cookie to satisfy your sweet tooth—with not too much guilt—this is it. Fully loaded with superfood goodness and just the right amount of sweet, these cookies make such a delicious treat! Everyone in my family loves them!

| YIELD: 24 cookies | PREP TIME: 15 minutes | COOK TIME: 40 minutes |
| --- | --- | --- |

## PROCEDURE

1. Preheat the oven to 350°F.

2. In a large bowl, combine the oats, flour, flaxseeds, brown sugar, chocolate chips, cranberries, dates, and cinnamon.

3. Mix in apple juice, olive oil, and vanilla.

4. Scoop one ounce of cookie dough and shape into round circles, or put into a small muffin pan.

5. Sprinkle with sesame seeds.

6. Bake for 40 to 45 minutes.

7. Cool completely.

8. Remove from baking sheet and store in an airtight container.

## INGREDIENTS

2 cups gluten-free old fashioned oats

1 cup gluten-free flour or almond meal

½ cup ground flaxseeds

¼ cup brown sugar

¼ cup chocolate chips

¼ cup dried cranberries

¼ cup chopped dates

½ teaspoon cinnamon powder

1 cup apple juice

¼ cup olive oil

1 teaspoon vanilla extract

1 tablespoon sesame seeds

# Sheila's Dark Chocolate Peppermint Bark

My friend and fellow yoga instructor Sheila Pinto brings this dessert to every Christmas gathering, and I look forward to it every year. I love the dark chocolate and peppermint combo. Who doesn't?

**YIELD:** 20 ounces peppermint bark    **PREP TIME:** 60 minutes    **COOK TIME:** 5 minutes

## PROCEDURE

1. Line a baking sheet with wax paper.

2. In a medium saucepan over low heat, melt the chocolate slowly, stirring continuously.

3. Once the chocolate is melted, add the peppermint drops. Taste and add more if you like.

4. Spread the chocolate evenly on the wax paper and top with the mint pieces.

5. Freeze for 30 to 60 minutes, uncovered, until the bark is solidly frozen.

6. Drop the baking sheet on your countertop to break the bark into pieces.

7. Decorate with more mints so the bark looks festive.

8. Serve with love.

## INGREDIENTS

20 ounces dark chocolate (the darker the better)

15 drops peppermint oil (I prefer the doTERRA brand), plus more as needed

6 mints or candy canes, crunched into small pieces, plus a few extra for decoration

# Nicole's Flourless Chocolate Cake

We often gather as a family at Sugar Bay, my parents' beach house, and we almost always have this cake. Nicole is a master in the kitchen and has been feeding our family and friends for over 20 years. She's a rockstar, and this cake is a winner. Top it with vanilla ice cream or Vegan Coconut Dream Cream Topping and go to heaven!

| YIELD: 8 (2-inch) slices | PREP TIME: 15 minutes | COOK TIME: 30 minutes |
|---|---|---|

## PROCEDURE

1. Preheat the oven to 325°F.

2. Place a large roasting pan in the oven. It should be big enough to hold an 8-inch round baking pan. Add enough water to come halfway up the sides of the baking pan.

3. Grease the baking pan with butter and line the bottom with wax paper.

4. Combine the butter and chocolate in a large heatproof bowl.

5. Fill a large skillet with water. Bring the water just to a simmer over medium-high heat.

6. Set the bowl over the barely simmering water and stir until the chocolate and butter are melted and smooth.

7. Remove from the heat and whisk in the egg yolks.

8. In another large bowl, beat the egg whites with a handheld mixer until they form soft peaks, about 5 minutes, adding the cream of tartar and sugar as you mix.

9. Use a rubber spatula to fold a quarter of the egg white mixture into the melted chocolate mixture.

10. Add the rest of the egg white mixture. Stir it into the chocolate mixture completely.

## INGREDIENTS

1 pound bittersweet chocolate, coarsely chopped

1¼ sticks salted butter (at room temperature), plus more for greasing the pan

5 large eggs, separated (at room temperature)

¼ teaspoon cream of tartar

2 tablespoons granulated sugar

11. Spread the batter evenly into the baking pan, and set it in the large roasting pan in the oven.

12. Bake for 30 minutes, or until a toothpick inserted in the center comes out clean.

13. Remove the cake from the oven and allow it to cool in a water bath (place the cake pan in a pan of cool water; the water should come up almost to the top of the cake pan).

14. Remove the cake from the baking pan, cover with plastic wrap, and put it in the fridge to cool.

15. Serve with vanilla ice cream or Vegan Coconut Dream Cream Topping (recipe follows).

# Vegan Coconut Dream Cream Topping

This is a great dairy-free topping that takes the place of whipped cream. And it's so much better than Cool Whip!

---

YIELD: 14 ounces          PREP TIME: 8 hours to chill bowl/coconut milk
+ 10 minutes

---

## PROCEDURE

1. Refrigerate a medium mixing bowl and the can of coconut milk for 8 hours.

2. Pour the coconut milk into the cold mixing bowl. Using an electric mixer on high speed, beat the milk for 7 to 8 minutes, until stiff peaks form.

3. Add the sugar and vanilla and beat for another minute.

4. Add more sugar to taste.

5. Store in the fridge until ready to serve. The topping will keep, refrigerated, up to 3 days.

## INGREDIENTS

1 (14-ounce) can unsweetened coconut milk

2 tablespoons granulated sugar, plus more as needed

1 teaspoon vanilla extract

# Isabel's Maca Truffles

I became friends with Isabel Tonelli when I spent a summer in Connecticut. Isabel is a raw food chef extraordinaire and does the most amazing three-day raw food cleanses. I was honored to lead a yoga and detox retreat with her, where I met her Maca Truffles. Needless to say, it was love at first bite, and she has generously shared her recipe.

**YIELD:** 60 truffles    **PREP TIME:** 10 minutes

## PROCEDURE

1. Pulse the cashews, 2 cups of the coconut, the dates, maca powder, maple syrup, vanilla, and salt together in a food processor until a sticky dough forms, about 3 minutes.

2. Form the dough into small, bite-size balls (approximately 1½ tablespoons of dough per ball).

3. Place the remaining ½ cup shredded coconut on a plate and roll the balls in the coconut to coat.

4. Store in a mason jar or other airtight container in the fridge or freezer. The balls will keep for up to a month.

## INGREDIENTS

2 cups raw cashew nuts

2½ cups sweetened shredded coconut, divided

2 cups pitted and chopped Medjool dates

1 tablespoon maca powder

3 tablespoons maple syrup

1 teaspoon vanilla extract

1 teaspoon Himalayan sea salt

# Victoria's Mango Bread

My high school and forever friend, foodie and *Miami Herald* food critic Victoria Pesce Elliott has been making this legendary Mango Bread for as long as I've known her (and that's a very long time). This recipe has been featured on TV and in numerous magazines, and I am so honored to have it in my book. Vix never shows up to your house without a loaf of her Mango Bread, wrapped artfully and tied with a bow. It's as sweet and as deep and magical and wonderful as she is! Make it when mangoes are in season and freeze. Be sure to carry on the tradition and give it to your friends.

| YIELD: 1 loaf | PREP TIME: 15 minutes | COOK TIME: 60 minutes |
| --- | --- | --- |

## PROCEDURE

1. Heat the oven to 350°F.

2. Grease a 9-by-5-inch loaf pan with oil and dust with flour; set aside.

3. Whisk the flour, baking soda, cinnamon, nutmeg, and salt in a large bowl; make a well in the center.

4. In a food processor or high-speed blender, puree 1 of the mangoes.

5. Whisk the oil, sugar, whole eggs, egg yolk, mango puree, and vanilla in a separate bowl.

6. Pour the mixture into the well in the dry ingredients and stir to combine the wet and dry ingredients thoroughly.

7. Fold in the diced mangoes, walnuts, and coconut and pour into the prepared pan.

8. Bake until a toothpick inserted into the bread comes out clean, 60 to 80 minutes.

9. Let cool and serve.

## INGREDIENTS

⅓ cup vegetable oil, plus more for greasing

1½ cups all-purpose flour, plus more for dusting

¾ teaspoon baking soda

1 teaspoon cinnamon

½ teaspoon ground nutmeg

½ teaspoon Himalayan sea salt

2 large very ripe mangoes, peeled, pitted, and cut into ¼-inch dice, divided

1 cup brown sugar

2 eggs

1 egg yolk

½ teaspoon vanilla extract

½ cup chopped walnuts

½ cup shredded unsweetened coconut

# TEN THINGS I DO TO
# STAY INSPIRED EVERY DAY

When I lead my seven-day transformational Live Fit Detox Programs, I have the opportunity to deeply connect with the people in my program and watch their physical, mental, and spiritual transformations. It is a beautiful thing. I always come back feeling so full of gratitude and motivated to keep sharing what I know and doing what I love to do most in the world: inspire others to see their greatness, their light, their magnificence, and their limitless potential! One of the questions I get asked all the time is what do I do to keep going, to keep being passionate—despite the years, the challenges, the setbacks—and to keep my inner light shining bright? Everyone needs a little inspiration, so I thought I would share the ten things I do daily to stay inspired.

## 1. Be Grateful for It All

I always end my yoga classes by saying something like this: Take a moment to be in the deepest of gratitude for every single thing in your life that has led you up to this moment. When you do this, you come fully in the present, where there is no worry about the past or fear of the future. It's a deeply powerful exercise. Please, do it every day.

## 2. Remember That Home Is Where the Heart Is

I always share in my yoga classes that you have to root down first before you rise up! To stay inspired, I make sure that my foundation—my root, my home life—is grounded and secure. As I wrote in the introduction, I had to sacrifice Shakti, the place I had created and loved with all my heart and soul, to move to Montego Bay for my family. If your home and your closest relationships are not happy, healthy, and grounded, you cannot step out into the world to spread your wings and fly! So every day I make sure all is good at home, with my husband, my children, the people who work for me, my parents, and my sisters. Once all is well and my home life is secure, I am ready to do my work.

### 3. Take My Hour of Power

This is my non-negotiable, sacred hour to myself in the early morning to move my body, breathe, stretch, relax, and meditate. This is where I get to clear my head, organize my thoughts, do something good for my body, and connect with my soul. Nothing comes between me and that hour! I really encourage you to find your Hour of Power and do something that makes you feel happy, fulfilled, and challenged to go out of your comfort zone. Make it a non-negotiable part of your life too.

### 4. Eat High-Vitality Food for the Temple

I believe with all my heart that the precious body God gave each of us is a Temple of the Divine, a temporary home for our soul. It is so important to honor and respect this temple by putting high-vitality, organic, unprocessed, clean foods into it to keep our souls shining bright. The day I started loving my body and treating it as a temple was the day my long struggle with weight issues and eating disorders stopped. I loved myself to health. Today my body is lean, agile, and full of energy! Get a positive start to each day with lemon water to flush out toxins, and drink a green power shake to stay alkaline. Eat a plant-based diet and follow the 80-10-10 rule 80 percent of the time. Love, accept, and honor your temple so much that you make healthy choices and see your body change.

### 5. Do Daily Yoga and Meditation

I honestly do not know where I would be without the gifts of yoga and meditation in my life. Yoga is a never-ending journey of self-discovery. Every time I get on the mat, I am able to see where in my life I'm not practicing my yoga, which means where I am not in union, or alignment with my higher truth. I use my breath, postures, and meditation to get back to that place of balance. It's never too late to try yoga; classes and studios are abundant. Find a class that works for you, come to one of my retreats, or sign up for my online 7-Day Journey of Transformation and learn about yoga and meditation practices; delicious, healthy detox food; and self-care techniques from the privacy of your own home. Or roll out your mat and let your body and breath guide you. Just do your yoga, even if it's five minutes a day. It's important!

## 6. Find People Who Inspire and Support Me

Do you know that you are the sum total of the five people you spend the most time with? I make sure those people I hang with, work with, follow on social media, or watch on TV are inspiring me to greatness, not bringing me down. I get inspired every day by women like Marie Forleo, Gabby Bernstein, and Kris Carr, who are all passionate about what they do and are making the world a better place. I read their blogs every day to stay on the cutting edge, and I regularly unsubscribe from those not serving me.

## 7. Give Back

Yes, as the Prayer of Saint Francis says, "it is in giving that we receive." I find a way to serve those who are less fortunate and give back—not for thanks or recognition, but to help those in need feel important and loved. I know it's hard with our own busy lives and dramas, but if you make the time, you will be so inspired by those you give to. They have so much to teach you.

## 8. Take Care of Myself

I come from a family of strong women who are natural-born givers. They put everyone else before themselves. I lived that way for years, but it was not long before I burned out badly! Today I live by Jim Rohn's motto: "I will take care of me for you, if you will take care of you for me" (Rohn was an American entrepreneur, author, and motivational speaker). Trust me, no one is going to take care of you, so you better learn to take care of yourself first, so you are strong and healthy enough to take care of those around you. My daily self-care practices, besides my Hour of Power, yoga, and a high-vitality diet, are skin brushing, oil pulling, aromatherapy, spending time on my BioMat, being out in nature, and most important, getting eight hours of sleep a night. When you make yourself a priority, others respect you more, and you respect and value yourself and your time more too.

## 9. Detox Often, Mentally and Physically

This is what I love about my detox program: it is so much more than a cleanse. It's about detoxing your mind and your life and letting go of those things that are no longer serving you. We are spiritual beings having a human experience for a very short time on earth. We change and we grow just like the plants and the trees. Every so often we need to pause, to prune or to uproot if the soil is no longer fertile. A true detox is a time to reassess your life and see if you are still living joyfully, peacefully, and lovingly, and if not, to do something about it. Life is too short. Let go of fear and release those things, people, habits, and careers that are no longer serving your highest good. Trust that when you do so, the universe will guide you to the place you need to be.

## 10. Make This Day the Best Day of Your Life

Yes, last but not least, I have found that the most detrimental thing I can do to myself is give energy to my negative thoughts. Instead, like my new friend and mentor, ninety-seven-year-old Tao Porchon-Lynch (the world's oldest living yoga master) says: "Wake up every day and say this is going to be the best day of my life." Do it! Since I met Tao in December 2014, I have been doing this every day, and I can feel the actual chemistry of my cells change with the charge of this powerful affirmation.

**So, my friends, there you have it:** ten things I do every day to keep my light shining bright. They take work and commitment, and many times I fail, but with practice and consistency these habits have become such a part of me that I don't know life any other way. I am able to catch myself when I'm dwelling in fear, doubt, or negative self-talk and bring myself back into balance and truth. You can too!

# Index